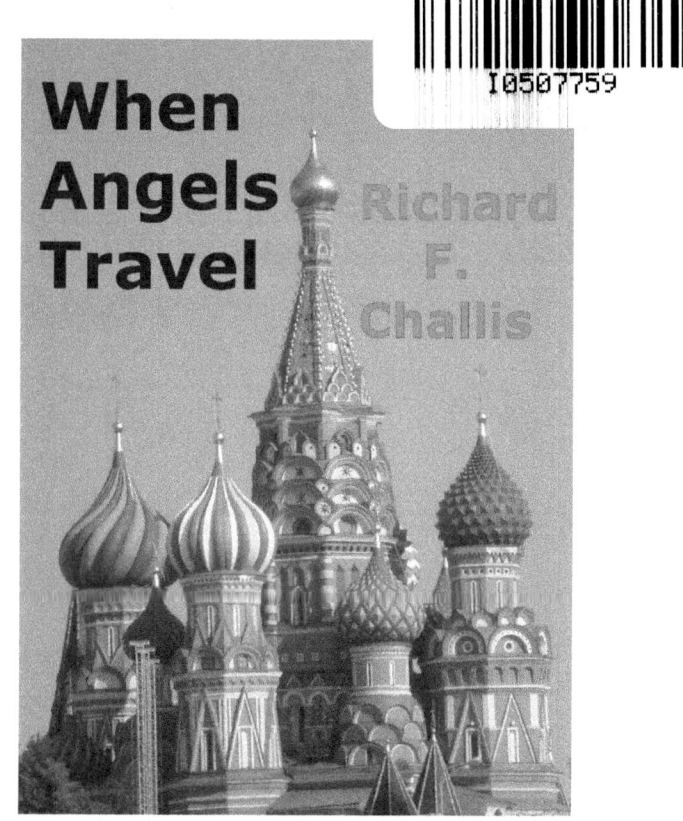

When Angels Travel

By Richard F. Challis

Copyright Richard F. Challis 1968

The publisher has the permission and approval of the copyright owners of this work to publish it.

Contents

Forward
Moscow
Paris
Germany
Switzerland
Pakistan:
India
Burma
Bankok
Saigon
Manila
Taiwan
Hong Kong
Seoul
Tokyo
UFO'S
Singapore
Malaysia
Djakarta
Australia
N.Z.
U.S.A
Epilogue

When Angels Travel

Foreword

This should have been called: "An Innocent Abroad". Mark Twain had no right to use the title since he was a journalist when he made his famous tour. I, on the other hand, was almost forty before I set out on my travels; until then I had not been outside Great Britain, and my longest sea trip was on the ferry across the Humber from Hull to Lincolnshire.

When I set out, Europe was enduring one of its bad summers, but for a time, good weather travelled with me, and a German acquaintance quoted: "Wenn Engel verreisen, scheint die Sonne" - "When Angels travel, the sun shines". This sounded so much more attractive than the alternative explanation: "The Devil looks after his own", that I felt I should use it - but really, this is the account of the travels of an innocent abroad.

When Angels Travel

Chapter 1 Moscow

"The use of travelling is to regulate imagination by reality, and instead of thinking how things may be, to see them as they really are."
(Samuel Johnson)

"Without going out of the door
One can know the whole world;
Without peeping out of the window
One can see the Tao of heaven.
The further one travels
The less one knows."
(From the Tao-Te King)

"You will not like it!" warned the Dutchman gloomily, as the K.L.M. plane started its descent on Moscow. Apart from a half hour in the Transit Lounge of Amsterdam Airport, this was to be my first landing on foreign soil. I thought that he was probably right; my ideas were vague but I expected something drab, utilitarian and depressing.

A somewhat severe Russian with whom I had negotiated a visa in London, had rather confirmed me in this view. Trying to build a strong case, I stressed that Machino-import in Moscow wanted me there for discussions and in fact had cabled naming the previous Monday as a convenient date.

"Then why were you not there?" asked the Russian, bleakly.

As we emerged from the plane a dour, uniformed Russian took my passport, gazed silently at the photograph in it and inspected me for what seemed a long time. I wanted to explain a number of things: that my good looks are of the elusive sort which no photographer has yet captured; that this was a particularly sloppy bit of photography; that although on the evidence of the picture I had recently had an outbreak of leprosy on my chin, this was merely an illusion caused by the maladroit use of photo-floods; that anyway, I have a beautiful nature. In silence, he allowed me to set foot on his country and soon I was jostling with two plane-loads of people, all trying to get through passport-control, customs and currency-exchange, where banking operations were being conducted with the aid of an abacus, - a frame of beads similar to one on which, many years ago, I had learned simple addition and subtraction. Here, though, the operators used them expertly to check involved calculations.

Soon, with three other visitors, I was speeding into Moscow in an Intourist car. True, the blocks of apartment-houses were lacking in appeal, but anyone who has seen Huddersfield on a wet November day is not afterwards disposed to be too critical. Darkness had fallen by the time I reached the heart of Moscow.

By the following night, I had a wealth of impressions to absorb. All senses had been assailed by things rich and strange. Two odours seemed prevalent: firstly, the slightly sickly scent of Russian tobacco which reminded me of some Finnish cigarettes I had once been foolish enough to tackle and which explained why so many Russians wanted British or American cigarettes; secondly, some difference - presumably in refining - gave exhaust fumes from Soviet cars a distinctive, all-pervading smell.

The sense of taste had been pleasantly surprised by its first acquaintance with vodka, sturgeon and caviar. I have often felt that it is a mistake to rush for the treats of this life. The setting is all-important. Thus, I tested my first caviar in the Hotel National, Moscow, overlooking the yellow-ochre walls and golden domes of the Kremlin. I was sharing a table with a Belgian who was a frequent visitor to Moscow. Learning that this was to be my first caviar, he rejected the initial serving and demonstrated how to check the colour and resilience to be sure it was good quality and fresh. I have had caviar since, in a number of places, but none the equal of that on my first night in Moscow.

Later during this tour, I was offered Kangaroo-tail soup but refused it, so that my first bowl was taken some thirty-thousand feet above the fantastic red desert heart of Australia, just as the pilot pointed out Alice Springs below us. Without these associations, how could I hope to keep fresh the memory of that bowl of Kangaroo-tail soup? Particularly as it tasted just like Ox-tail! But caviar - that is a different matter! The food in the main Moscow hotels is good and well-cooked, providing you will eat the Russian dishes. An American tourist who was complaining because she could not have cold turkey, no doubt went home with a different impression.

With less than ten days' notice of this visit to Moscow my Russian language studies were not advanced. I could count up to four, say "Please", "Thank you", "Yes", "No", "Pleased to meet you", or recite the first quarter of their telephone alphabet - ("Ah, Anna, Beh Boris, Veh Vasili, fieh Grigori") - but no more. Although the hotels have a Service-Bureau where the main European languages are spoken, English is not yet widely known. The obliging Belgian had taught me enough Russian so that I could order breakfast in my room - tea, toast, butter and a boiled egg. The egg arrived almost raw and on the second morning I added a second egg and specified "four minutes". Russian minutes are apparently about half the length of British ones and it was not until I had increased the time to six minutes that I had a properly boiled egg.

Intourist had put me in the Hotel Pekin which is solid, clean and Victorian. Apart from breakfast, I ate mainly at the Hotel National, partly because of difficulty with the Pekin's menus, which were in Russian only, but also because the National was more convenient. I enjoyed the walk from the one to the other along the wide and handsome Gorky Street, which accommodates up to twelve lines of traffic. I had been told, by friends who had never been there, that there is very little traffic in Moscow. After I had been almost run down several times by this non-existent traffic, I decided that I had been misled. I spent a few foolish minutes trying to cross the vast expanse of Manejnaya Square, with traffic shooting at me unpredictably and policemen blowing whistles and waving furiously - before discovering that the entrance down to the Metro also gave access to a subway under the square.

I had been warned that all traffic travels on the right and a little preliminary practice along part of the East Lancs road, coming out of Liverpool, had already convinced me that it is shockingly dangerous - I was nearly killed! Fortunately, I did little driving throughout this tour, but as a pedestrian I invariably glanced the wrong way before stepping into the road.

A telephone call from my hotel room had established that my initial interview with Machino-import would be the following morning and so my first day in Moscow was given over to sightseeing.

Every schoolboy knows that Moscow's climate is extreme and that in late August it will be hot. This knowledge did not prevent a feeling of surprise when I found it hot and sunny, with temperatures in the eighties. Subconsciously, I suppose I was still expecting snowdrifts, troikas and wolves. Surprise, too, was my immediate reaction on seeing a road-mending gang of women, handling road-rollers, picks and shovels - but a moment's reflection convinced me that this was as it should be. Man was made for finer things than shovelling rubble. As I walked respectfully past these Amazons, a young Muscovite fell in step with me.

"You wish to buy genuine, antique, holy Russian ikons?" he asked. "You come with me to my apartment, I show you valuable ikons!"

Probably he had made them himself the previous day; in any event, it did not seem a good idea to visit his apartment. "I'm afraid I cannot," I began.

"You afraid? Why you afraid?" he asked, looking apprehensively over his shoulder.

"No, I mean I am sorry I cannot."

Shortly afterwards, another young Russian wanted to buy my shirt, a nylon waterproof if I had one, or to introduce me to his sister.

He did not look the sort of young man who would have a sister and I had no intention of going into business in Moscow, but it was refreshing to find, unsubdued, human nature in all its splendid, shifty, sinfulness.

The U.S.S.R. does not yet appear to be releasing nylon for clothing. Although the average Muscovite is clean and decently dressed, the styling and material of their clothes instantly proclaim the visiting Westerner and lead to illegal offers from "spivs". Long, long overdue is an epic poem justifying the ways of the 'spiv", the "con-man", the "grafter", the "fiddler", the "wide-boy". At considerable personal risk they devote to their shifty callings an amount of ingenuity, daring and inventiveness which applied to one of the legally established forms of trickery would give them riches and honours. But the true "spiv" cannot cross the line into normal business thievery. The thrill of the game, the calculated risk, the pitting of his abilities against the weight of society - these are what he lives for.

In the golden August sunshine, the centre of Moscow looked spacious, serene and even graceful. The magnificent squares seem as large as one of the smaller English counties. A child was feeding pigeons near the splendidly barbaric and many-coloured St. Basil's Cathedral. The yellow-ochre tinted walls and the golden domes of the Kremlin under the bright sun added to the general effect of colour and charm.

I had a job of selling to do. The buyer was to be Machino-import, the State Board which buys certain categories of foreign equipment for factories anywhere in the U.S.S.R.

The Deputy-Chairman, with whom I was involved, was virtually the sole buyer of my type of equipment for a nation of over 200 million people. If I could not do business with him, there was no other customer in the whole of the U.S.S.R.

The Deputy-Chairman had two technical assistants with him. He spoke good English, which was fortunate since, apart from my ordering a breakfast from him, we could have achieved nothing in Russian. As the tour progressed, I felt increasingly guilty over the language problem. Regularly, prominent businessmen or trade-journals nag at us and insist that if we wish to sell abroad, we must pay our customers the compliment of learning their language. The point sounds good but it is difficult to apply. Within a week, later on, I would have needed to be fluent in Malay, Thai and Burmese. English is the first or second language of the world and is handled with precision and elegance by people from many countries. The Pakistani in Karachi, who said to me: "Now we go to meet Mr ---. He is an Englishman like yourself and a great scoundrel; you will get on well with him" - clearly was in no need of further English lessons. As a polite compromise, I tried to learn a few words of greeting, thanks and farewell in each language.

With the Deputy-Chairman of Machino-import and his assistants, I spent several hours clarifying technical points. We broke off at one point to stand in silence for a few moments while a funeral procession passed, with solemn music, along the street below us.

It was, explained the Deputy-Chairman, the funeral of his former chief. We adjourned until the next-but-one day. There had been no mention of price and the real battle was still to come.

And then - it was all over and I was enjoying an Aeroflot breakfast (which started with caviar) on my way back to Amsterdam, and buying gift pots of caviar, miniature bottles of vodka, bracelets and other souvenirs from the attractive hostesses. Meetings with Machino-import, over a period of eight days, had produced some hard bargaining down to the limit of my concessions. Pyrrus is remembered for the Battle of Asculum, ("Another victory like that and we're done for.") I had no wish to be remembered by my Company for a Pyrric Sale. I had heard stories of businessmen in Moscow who had bluffed an order from the Russians by packing and booking a flight as though determined to leave. This did not happen to me - perhaps there was something not quite right about the way I packed.

If I did not have an order in my suitcase, at least I had all thirty-two of Beethoven's Piano Sonatas on fourteen long-play records, performed by Soviet pianists. I had learned that, like many cultural or educational materials, records were cheap - about ten shillings each and so I made my way into a record-shop on Gorky Street. No English was spoken and my phrase-book did not help much, but when I saw on a box the figures 32 and the Russian word for Beethoven, 1 needed to look no further.

I also had memories and programmes of two performances of the Stanislavsky Ballet (of which Tchaikovsky was once a Director) - which included Russian words which by that time I was capable of discovering that these were Don Juan and Scheherazade.

".... and two dolls and some caviar and some L.P's and some miniature vodka", I continued, while the Customs officer at London Airport gave me a swift, practised glance to see whether I was stupid or merely pretending to be. You cannot fool them - a quick scrawl on my baggage and I was through.

Chapter 2 Paris

"I wish he would not go to Paris," said Miss Matilda anxiously. "I don't believe frogs will agree with him; he used to have to be very careful what he ate, which was curious in so strong-looking a young man."
(Cranford - Mrs. Gaskell)

I returned to London only to collect a Burmese visa which had just been confirmed and in three days I was on my way to Paris - for my first visit. Within ten minutes of my arrival, I had managed to get myself kidnapped.

The loudspeaker at Le Bourget Airport was asking "Monsieur Shalleece" to go to the transit desk. As I approached expectantly, a man came to me with outstretched hand and announced: "Fenwick!" (The name, surprisingly enough, of the large French factory I was visiting.) I said: "Heureux de faire votre connaissance" -I had been practicing this all the way from London and was rather pleased with the way I got it off.

Within minutes we were driving briskly along the road into Paris. He told me that his name was Dreyfus and I repressed a stupid impulse to ask him how he had enjoyed Devil's Island.

Even allowing for the fact that his English was not much better than my French, we quickly seemed to be at cross-purposes. When it became obvious that there was a mistake somewhere, he stopped and we re-introduced ourselves. He had not said "Fenwick.' but "Fenwick?" - because he was there to meet a Mr. Fenwick from England, whereas I was expecting to be met by someone from the French Company of that name.

Laughing heartily, my kidnapper turned and drove back to the airport where we parted with expressions of mutual esteem.

For almost forty years, Paris had been a city known to me only through my reading, and ghosts peopled the streets so familiar by name.

Boswell dismissed Paris in a few words: "approached Paris; Invalides appeared as St. Paul's does, coming to London. Was not affected much." Next day, January 13th, 1766, he added: "No change of ideas from being in Paris

A friend drove me around and obligingly translated place-names into English, so that Sacré Coeur became "Holy Heart", and I had, mentally, to translate back into French before I knew what I was looking at. The same friend said: When you do not know a French word, pronounce the English as though it were French, and nine times out of ten you will either be correct or be understood."

Later, it occurred to me that this advice might create misunderstandings, as I wanted to know when the news came on T.V. and was searching my memory for the French for "news". I might have found myself asking at what hour the nudes appeared, (les nues). Probably it would not have mattered; our drive took us through Montmartre where every other place was a strip-joint.

Approaching the Louvre, the next day, I was gratified to be offered indecent photographs. No doubt the man was employed by the Bureau of Tourism to ensure that visitors are not disappointed in their expectations, just as the drunks I was to see rolling around the New York Bowery at noon, were undoubtedly there to provide local colour.

Paris is a fine and beautiful city. The horse chestnut trees along the Champs Elysees were spilling "conkers" profusely. I pocketed two which had burst from their cases at my feet, fly stained and varnished, and eventually used them in Australia to demonstrate the game of "conkers".

"A dinner without cheese is like a day without sunshine", quoted my French host as he selected four varieties from the fifteen or so on the cheeseboard. France is justly noted for its cheeses and in general is a death-trap for the gastronome.

Two meals, at Le Grand Veneur and at a restaurant with the fascinating name of Les Anysestiers du Roy will linger in my memory along with the recollection of a tripe and cow—heel pie I shared with an alleged friend in Lancashire - but for different reasons.

Prices, not merely of meals, are high, and a shopping expedition produced only the melancholy reflection that apparently, I could afford nothing. An attempt to buy lingerie ended when the critical measurements, which I had carefully memorised, proved useless because they were in inches. My efforts at instant conversion into centimetres produced results which could not possibly be the measurements of any human female, however unfortunate, and the shop-assistant, like so many more, spoke no English and apparently understood no French.

I hesitated a moment outside a window advertising individual eyelashes. Probably I could manage the price of one, but whom did I know, short of an eyelash?

My last whole day was a Saturday and as the weather was kind, I was able to carry out a project of seeing Paris, on foot. The route from my hotel in the Avenue D'Iena was planned to give me a few hours at the Louvre and at the Galerie du Jeu de Paume where most of the Louvre's Impressionist paintings are hung.

I saw the originals of paintings familiar to me as reproductions and felt that I had not been misled except when the original was massive in size, like the fragment of Monet's "D'ejeuncr Sur L'Herbe", which turned out to be about fourteen feet high - a fairly substantial fragment!

The magnificent cathedral of Notre Dame, seen first by moonlight and floodlight, displayed its Gothic splendour to great advantage, but even in the sunshine it retained its impact. Surely, high up, the face and figure of Quasimodo could be seen - and, in the shadows, the Archdeacon for ever slips from his desperate handhold on the gargoyle, two hundred feet up. And the beautiful Esmeralda? "All at once the man at the gibbet kicked away the ladder with his heel, and Quasimodo, who for some moments had not breathed, saw swinging from the end of the rope, about two yards from the ground, the unfortunate girl, with the man crouched upon her shoulders.

The rope twisted around several times and Quasimodo saw the girl writhe with horrible contortions."

Those of us too squeamish to re-read Hugo's novel can take heart. Quasimodo's eyes must have deceived him, or someone else was hanged in error, for nestling in the shadow of Notre Dame Cathedral I found "Esmeralda's Cafe". Strangely enough, some months previously, when passing through Haworth, the Brontes' birthplace, I had seen "Heathcliff's Cafe". It is a comforting thought that after their trials and tribulations, famous characters should be able to settle down to serving tea and cakes to the tourists. At first, I felt that Heathcliff's grim and forbidding temperament would not be conducive to success, but in Yorkshire, as J.B. Priestley has said, civility is still regarded with suspicion as something hypocritical and unmanly, so no doubt Heathcliff has prospered.

I did not go into Esmeralda's Cafe'. She might have turned into a strident hag, serving cold coffee in dirty cups, and I could not have borne that. No, on reflection Hugo was right - it was better to hang her.

Chapter 3 Germany

As a young man, I had for a couple of terms, studied German at evening classes. My father-in-law retired and in Search of occupation decided to come too. The teacher was Mr. Reinach, a refugee from Hitler's Third Reich. He was a purist in the use of language and although only recently resident in England, his English was immaculate. Only once did he slip, when he said: "a lustful boy", meaning "a lusty boy", and from some polite smirks on a few faces he realised that he had made a mistake and asked for synonyms. These were promptly provided by the class and ranged from "lecherous" –my own offering -to "randy" from a demure-looking young lady who should not have known what we were talking about.

That same evening, he was carefully explaining to my father-in-law who had failed to grasp it earlier, the intricacies of case and number in respect of nouns and pronouns. Knowing my father-in-law, I could tell that he was not listening, but had dropped into the private world of the elderly. After Mr. Reinach's masterly summary, taking probably twenty minutes, my father-in-law said: "I'm afraid I shall never 'get' all that – but if you can teach me a sort of pidgin-German, that will do me.

The look on Mr. Reinach's face lives in my memory and has afforded me many a quiet chuckle over the years.

But the same years had largely robbed me of the slender results of two terms. As we circled Dusseldorf for over an hour, waiting for ground-fog to lift, I mentally raked among the ashes and came up with a few unpromising items. While not quite in the position Negley Farson, who started his Arabic studies with: "The eunuch is in the garden of the Caliph" - my stock of German seemed just as remote from everyday life. I could still tell the story of Little Red-Riding-Hood, recite a German version of there's a hole in my bucket", announce that "the East wind is bitter cold today", refuse a cigarette or ask for a copy of the Radio-Times. And then a mental fog closed in, but below, the mist had cleared and we landed in sunshine.

The Export manager of the German firm I was visiting had brought his eighteen-year-old daughter with him to meet me, setting a standard which subsequent hosts around the world failed to live up to, for she was as fresh and beautiful as the morning itself. In Australia, later, I shared the back seat of my host's car with his large dog, which under a pretence of playfulness, was trying to sink his fangs into my jugular artery while I, simulating friendship, tried to throttle him. The Australian said that the dog and I were "real cobbers" but the dog knew better.

My hotel at Velbert displayed a letter from Bismarck, acknowledging with thanks a comfortable stay there. This was for me, a new light on one of the characters from my history books; I had never associated the "Iron Chancellor" with this sort of small civility. Certainly, it was a very clean and comfortable hotel and if I almost received drei Martini instead of dry, this was entirely my own fault. As Velbeit is near Essen, I had expected a grimy, industrial setting and was pleasantly surprised by green and rolling hills. But this is not part of the tourist's Germany; here are no castles, gorges or Rhine-maidens. The Rhine is wide and purposeful as it flows across a plain, with Dusseldorf on its right bank.

Business kept me too busy for sight-seeing, but one evening I saw a most respectable strip-tease act, selected by my host because he wanted to include his wife and daughter in the outing. Certainly, there was nothing to shock them; the stripper at the end of her act would still have been considered ever-dressed on many beaches. Feeling, perhaps, that this had been dull fare, my host mimed a strip-tease of his own – provocatively taking off imaginary stockings and throwing them coyly at us; unclipping an imaginary brassiere and turning his back to us as he whipped it off, then holding it exultantly aloft by a non-existent strap as he turned to face, us.

It was the best night-club entertainment I on the tour. His plump and jolly wife almost shook the room with her laughter; his daughter gave the indulgent smile with which the young view the antics of their parents.

During my final afternoon and evening, I visited Wuppertal which has a monorail suspension railway dating back to 1898, giving a bird's-eye view of the countryside and congestion-free travel to and from the town. On the way to Dusseldorf, I saw the name Neanderthal on a signpost and asked if this was the site of the relics of Neanderthal Man, since, apart from assuming it was in central Europe, it had never occurred to me to wonder where Neanderthal was. My colleague not only confirmed this but obligingly turned off the main road so that we could go through the museum; he had been intending to go there himself but had lived in the vicinity a bare quarter of a century, so he had not had time. There had been much rain and the lane from the road to the museum, through a wood, was dank and marshy. The 70,000-year-old bones were there, looking more like something the dog had not bothered to bury than the remains of a remote ancestor. There were cave paintings from France and Spain together with other relevant material, all well displayed in a smart museum.

In Dusseldorf we walked along the broad Kaiser Allee, photographed each other against the background of the Rhine and, finished the evening with beer, schnaps and a meal at an inn.

My colleague was taking his schnaps medicinally, for a cold, he told me, though this did not involve any discernible difference in the method of drinking it. Everyone I had spoken to in Germany had a thick cold - no doubt the wretched weather was responsible. The sunshine which had arrived with me had been extinguished and rain was falling from leaden skies. We sat silently with glasses in front of us, looking out into the gloom

I felt perfectly at home.

Chapter 4 Switzerland

From Dusseldorf I flew to Zurich. At this stage all airlines were new to me and I eagerly read their magazines, full of chatty features such as "Meet your Captain", in which the writer had tried (too hard) to make the aircrews sound safe, solid, experienced, happily-married, well-adjusted and reliable. A parody would read something like this:

One of our most, senior Captains is the ever-popular, Australian born 'Baldy' Walters - a familiar figure to regular travellers on our jet-lines. 'Baldy' is laughingly reticent regarding his age but gives a clue by revealing that he flew for the R.F.C. in 1915 and for the R.A.A.F. afterwards, where he was known as 'Wheels up' Walters through a habit of landing before lowering the undercarriage.

After a crash had put him out of the Air Force, he came to England to get in on civil aviation. Asked about the difference between planes then and now, 'Baldy' gave us his flying philosophy in a few words: 'There's no real difference', he claims. 'The jets are faster and you've got to show the cow who's in charge!'

Baldy confesses to a liking for his 'grog' and has some amusing stories of 'beat-ups' in airport bars all over the world When he lived in Australia, his main sport was kangaroo shooting before he took to glasses. 'Now', he says in his blunt way, 'I'd have to club the 'roo and it would have to big bastard before I saw it!'

Captain Walters has eight children, all in the custody of their mothers, he hopes to be going on the jet conversion course soon, but because of the great popularity of our 'Golden Wonder' Jet Service, he is already flying them on a temporary basis."

And always there is a piece about a hostess; so sweet, so winsome, so wholesome, so safe.

Babs Meredith - 'Butterfingers' to her friends (Once, I dropped a baby'!!') - is an attractive, vivacious brunette. She says, she has Spanish blood in her family tree, and thinks this accounts for her flashing dark eyes and hot temper. She is sure she will enjoy the life once she has got her 'air-legs'. 'So embarrassing,' she says, "Why, the other day, I was sick all over a first-class passenger.'"

Fortunately, I was in Switzerland only a couple of days. Even in this short period I had acquired a reputation as a sort of mixture of Norman Wisdom and Jacques Tati. It started walked into, and very nearly through, a glass door in my company's offices in Zug. The crash of my face against the glass attracted the attention of all the typists in the general office. My glasses slipped askew down my nose, giving me a drunken, rakish appearance. Though half stunned, I managed to continue into the office and sit down at my desk a truly British performance.

Perhaps this had jarred my wits. At any rate, within an hour I had walked into the ladies toilet, which was luckily vacant at that moment under the impression that it was the door leading to the Vice-President's suite. Laughter from the outside and the fact that I was obviously not in the Vice-President's suite, made me aware of my error and I shot the bolt on the door and sat down for a few seconds to summon up the necessary courage to emerge. This I did, walking unhurriedly to my desk and even smiling vaguely at one of the girls who made a noise like an empty soda siphon and buried face in her hands.

Later that afternoon, I had unaccountably managed to smear ballpoint ink over my face and did not discover it until washing prior to leaving for the day. I had mistakenly assumed that the hilarity and difficulty in keeping straight faces, which afflicted the girls when they saw me, related to my earlier exploits.

Zug is a charming little town in the smallest of the Cantons. Many corporations maintain financial offices there, giving it a prosperity and international flavour independent of the tourist trade. My hotel room overlooked the ancient square and three nearby chiming clocks mark the passing of the quarter hours, day and night - but particularly at night, according to my impression. There was also a disagreement between them regarding the exact moment of the quarters, so that the sleepless visitor is assured of plenty of cheerful noise throughout the night.

As I was packing for departure, a fellow guest, an American, interrupted me for a moment with one of the problems created for us by modern technology. The plug on his electric shaver was a moulded-on type, new to me. The flex had frayed and broken away, just where it entered the plug and he was confronted with a service problem but no means of shaving. If the old-fashioned type of plug, made in halves held together by screws, had been fitted he could have carried out the repair in two minutes. He borrowed my battery-electric shaver and over breakfast later, we agreed that progress takes such strange forms that often, but for the advertising, we would not know it for progress at all.

Chapter 5 Karachi

"I ask myself: what to do about my carrier? It is a haddock!" During the three days we had been together, I had frequently admired the vivid English of this Pakistani salesman, but slight differences in stress, intonation and vowel sounds made close concentration necessary if I wanted to follow him all the time. As he had embarked on the story of his life, I had allowed my attention to wander and was now caught with this haddock.

After listening carefully and interposing a discreet question or two, I established that what he had actually said was: "I ask myself; what to do about my career? It is a headache!" We were outside Karachi on a rough, dirt track, jolting and bouncing around in a jeep. When I cautiously hinted that this was not the best of roads, the Pakistani explained that we were in the bed of a river, which most of the time is bone-dry and is then graded into some semblance of a road for use by quarry vehicles which were busily carting away sand and gravel. It seemed unlikely that water ever flowed here. Burning sands, blue sky and the sun beating powerfully down, gave me the illusion of being in a vast desert, rather than within a dozen miles of the centre of Karachi.

The annual rainfall is about five inches, though many locals refuse to believe that there is so much, and Karachi lives on water from the Indus.

It is a fascinating city, growing rapidly and changing rapidly. At this point in its transition, several centuries exist side by side, but in a few years the old will have disappeared and Karachi will be a duller city. In wide, modern streets, flanked by now multi-storey buildings, camels wend their way among hooting taxis and cars. In old Karachi, tiny ponies, harnessed side by side, with trappings jingling to their dainty trotting, pull little carts with big loads. Beggars and traders crowd the market area; multitudes of swarthy faces beneath a fiery sun.

There are several good hotels, but the Karachi Intercontinental is generally considered the best, as well as the most expensive. In air-conditioned luxury its guests eat, drink and sleep well. It is redeemed from being just another American hotel on foreign soil by its staff, in native costumes, and by the first-class local food available. There is a swimming pool where guests can bask in the perpetual sunshine.

On one of my evenings there, a reception was being given for the visiting head of a neighbouring State, and security guards, brandishing revolvers and automatic weapons, prowled the lobby. I have an aversion to gunmen, whatever their excuse. Probably an innocent action such as reaching for a fountain-pen, would have been misconstrued by some trigger-happy thug, and I decided to dine at the hotel opposite.

The "floor-show" consisted of a belly-dancer whose speciality it was to dance non-stop for forty-five minutes to the deafening accompaniment of about sixty watts of over-amplification. Her act was disappointing, but I was assured by a fellow diner that ten years previously she had been "terrific". Though I had a book in my pocket, politeness in a foreign city prevented me from reading. This was probably as well, because as a grand finale, the dancer leapt on to the tables bordering the room and pranced along them, and I would undoubtedly have had my fingers trodden on. The applause was almost as prolonged as the act. The dancer moved around, stopping to face anyone who seemed apathetic, and indicating by a glare and an imperious toss of the head that, she was entitled to better applause than that. I clapped; my hands were quite sore.

"Pan" for chewing can be bought ready-made at roadside stalls, but the well-to-do, many of whom chew in private, prepare their own. An evening meal with a Pakistani family ended with the preparation of pan by the wife - an elaborate ritual involving the smearing of the betel leaves with lime, camphor, areca-nut parings and other nameless substances, and the wrapping of this into a chewable wad. It was somewhat reminiscent of the elderly English lady's fussing with rows of caddies in the blending and preparation of her pot of tea.

I accepted a pan and found it larger than expected; it certainly inhibited conversation for a time. One of the ingredients colours the lips, tongue, saliva and eventually the teeth too, a bright red, which accounts for the sight of Pakistanis in the street apparently spitting out great gouts of blood, as well as for the red and fearsome smiles of many chewers. If the pan contains tobacco, it is necessary to spit, hence the occasional spittoon in office or home, but ours were tobacco-free. While coping with the unfamiliar package in my mouth, I swallowed a nut which felt like a razor-sharp five-jack and cut a series of grooves down my gullet.

The lady of the house had just returned from a pilgrimage to Mecca. This, of course, is something every Muslim hopes to achieve, but because of the shortage of foreign exchange a limited number may go and these are selected each year by lottery from all applicants. As she described the pilgrimage it sounded regrettably over-commercialised and reminded me of the comment that "Christmas would be all right if they didn't insist on dragging religion into it".

The taxi-driver had not set his meter, but I did not notice this until we had reached the Embassy of the U.S.A.

I pointed it out and the driver gave me a red-toothed smile. "I not set meter for friend! You are my friend - you pay me three rupees, four rupees, five, maybe!"

"I pay you two rupees," I said, "and that's too much." It was; a second journey to the Embassy next day cost less than a rupee.

The Embassy has an efficient and comprehensive commercial section, staffed by Americans and Pakistanis. One of the Americans dashed around for me very energetically and helpfully. He was a likeable man of the type often referred to as a "human dynamo". Perhaps he also rather conveyed the impression that he believed this to be the way an American should behave and that until something burst, he was determined to keep up the pace, He finally whisked me upstairs for a drink of 7-up and expatiated on the advantages of this canteen as we waited for our cold drinks.

"Make use of it any time at all," he said generously. "You can have coffee or a sandwich, prepared by our own staff and know that you're not going to pick up any bug here."

While he was speaking, I watched one of the Pakistani canteen staff, tearing meat from a chicken carcase with his fingernails, and making sandwiches with the results.

"Or if you want ice in your drink," continued my friend, "why, you can be sure it was made with water that isn't going to give you an upset stomach."

Pat to his cue, the attendant picked up ice with his fingers and dropped it in our drinks.

I walked from the Embassy to the "Chicken Inn" at the Metropole, a few hundred yards away, for lunch. Just as I had crossed the road a crack like a revolver shot made me jump. Two more followed before I realised that a boy with large, soulful eyes was demonstrating a whip.

"You buy!" he said, cracking it dangerously close to my ear. "Best camel-leather - only twelve rupees.'

I do not have the slightest need for a whip, but it was beautifully made, cheap at the pound he was asking and I felt safer with it in my hands than in his. After bargaining down to ten rupees, I bought it and also a newspaper from one of the interested crowd which had gathered. Then, camel-whip and newspaper in hand, I entered the hotel for lunch.

All visitors to Karachi are expected to have a ride on a camel and so I complied with the custom despite some inner reservations. I was not impressed; the centre of gravity seems too high, it under-steers and the brakes fade badly. For no known reason, my beast broke into a trot and hauling back on the reins produced little effect because of its long, flexible neck. Similarly, pulling on the offside rein in an attempt to turn right, brought the camel's head round until we were looking each other in the eye, but still he continued his forward motion. I could well understand why Lawrence of Arabia is said to have preferred being photographed with camels, to riding them.

Sometime after leaving Karachi I received a letter from my Pakistani friend:

"As promised, I was at the airport to see you off, but unfortunately I did not reach the counter until 7.17. You can imagine my disappointment and I confess that it had a very sickening effect on me. It so happened that my scooter was out of order and much to my surprise there was no taxi available nearby. I had to catch a bus immediately and after travelling half a mile I hurriedly got down and was able to hire a cab which, in spite of good endeavour, could not reach airport before 7.17. I had a feeling that I might still be in time as you had told me that you may be called in at 7.30. I am at fault, but had all the desire to be with you."

Chapter 6 Lahore

My one evening in the ancient city of Lahore was spent in the cinema, watching "The Last Time I Saw Paris". I had seen this film many years ago and recalled that a critic at the disliked both the film, and the choice of romantic hero, had commented unkindly on the glycerine tears trickling over Van Johnson's honest, wholesome, freckled but unromantic countenance. Now I was to see them again, though from politeness, not choice.

The young Pakistani who took me, averaged three visits weekly to the cinema and his uncritical enthusiasm for "the pictures" reminded me of my own youthful addiction. He assured me that the cinema was air-conditioned, but apparently attached his own meaning to the phrase for we sweltered, high up in the balcony, while a few ceiling-fans revolved in a tired fashion, as though exhausted by the heat. But my friend made amends the following day, Sunday, when he took me on a sight-seeing tour.

In a temperature of a hundred, we slogged up a minaret of Lahore's great mosque, claimed to be the largest in the world and to be capable of accommodating a hundred thousand worshippers at prayer at the same time, with room for each to prostrate himself. Two hundred feet below us, water-buffaloes were being hosed down. They would prefer to spend the heat of the day submerged, except for nostrils and eyes in a river or mud hole, but as working beasts had to accept this substitute. From the Mosque we moved on to the Fort of Akbar, pausing at the foot to refresh ourselves with warm lemonade before scaling its heights. We contemplated the graceful symmetry of the Shalimar Gardens, still maintained as in the days of the Mogul Emperors.

Despite Lahore's antiquity, it is a thriving city, the next in size to Karachi and the capital of the province of West Pakistan. It is a city of considerable charm, and it is a pity that apparently, it will for ever be linked in my memory with the mournfully banal air: "The Last time I saw Paris."

Chapter 7 Dacca

Hotel S----- is the best hotel in Dacca, capital of East Pakistan. As I waited to register, an American, with raised voice was telling the Manager what he thought of the hotel and its of survival once the new Inter-Continental Hotel was completed. The Manager, a young, good-looking Pakistani, emerged from the encounter with credit and dignity.

"Why," I wondered later, "do tourists get so worked up over trifles? This is an old-style hotel; the dining-room is gay with white-and-red uniformed waiters, swarthy, bearded and turbaned; the headwaiter has an engaging smile and a patriarchal beard some three square feet in area; the doorman is a midget with large, soulful eyes; a four-piece string and percussion ensemble plays music of the 1890's, giving the illusion of a recession in Time as well as a shift in Space; barefoot porters trot around with suitcases, briefcases, or hatboxes perched on their heads; everything so strange and fascinating! Why criticise it for not being a different sort of hotel?"

Towards midnight, when I was trying to fall asleep, it occurred to me that this business of "old style" could be overdone. In practical terms it meant that the hotel had been built to allow maximum circulation of air, for coolness. This, inevitably, gives maximum amplification of noise, and Goodman or Wharfedale would instantly have recognised and approved of the design principles. If someone on the ground floor coughed, it could be heard throughout all floors. A large proportion of the population of Dacca apparently lives in the corridors of the hotel, and I judged that in different parts of the corridor were being held a political meeting, a religious campaign, preliminary heats of the Asian Games and - immediately outside my door - the "Noisiest Men in Dacca" contest.

By one in the morning, the tumult and the shouting had died. I adjusted my head on the pillow and started, mentally, to recite the last section of "Lycidas", from "Weep no more, woeful shepherds". For an examination I had committed this to memory two decades ago and I have since found it far superior to counting sheep, as a soporific. Then the dogs began to bark. There were six or seven of them, sometimes working independently, sometimes in concert. They were galloping around the grounds and into a new, unfinished wing of the hotel, adjacent to my room.

In the morning, I tackled the Manager.

"Why, yes'. I too heard dogs!" he said, clearly happy to be able to confirm a guest's story. When I had enlarged on my feelings, he promised that he would "complain" - to the dogs no doubt. The two following nights were just as bad, but at least, I reflected, summoning as much philosophy as I could muster, there is nothing new in all this. As long ago as July 1st, 1667, Samuel Pepys was noting in his diary: "Up betimes, about 4. o'clock, by a damned noise between a sowgelder, and a cow and a dog, nobody after we were up being able to tell us what it was".

East Pakistan, separated from the West "Wing-by over a thousand miles of India, is about the same size as England, and with its population of 60 millions is one of the most heavily populated countries in the world. Much of the year it is hot and humid. It is a green and watery place, plagued by cyclones and attendant floods. The mighty "Father Brahmaputra" and his tributaries provide a network of waterways of great commercial value. The main language is Bengali as distinct from Urdu in West Pakistan, but in both "Wings" English is spoken widely and well.

In Dacca I met a local journalist, who interrogated me on some of the more abstruse points of Shakespearean drama and wanted to know whether I considered that Shakespeare thought of himself as a "man of his time or a man writing for and belonging to future times".

In England I would probably have been tempted to answer: "That's a very interesting question. Now, would you mind telling me what the hell it means!" - but courtesy here required that I struggle through to some sort of answer. At school he had read Shakespeare first in a simplified English Version, then in the original and had played Desdemona to his friend's Othello in a school production. During my stay, the two of them insisted on taking me to an entertainment by foreign artists - a rage event. There was some initial confusion about whether we would be seeing a ballet dancer or a belly dancer, but this was cleared up when we learned that we were to see a Soviet Cultural Group.

Apart from my main business in Dacca, I had to investigate an enquiry I had received in the post, from a firm with an impressive name - let us call them Trans-Orient Traders, in the hope that no firm with this title exists. I was having some difficulty in locating them. Taxis had twice put me down in the commercial heart of Dacca, taken their fare and departed before I could discover that I was not where I wanted to be. Policemen knew no English, and shops where I enquired pointed vaguely towards the north. At last I was put down by Fakirapool Bazaar and started to search for Trans-Orient Traders.

Their address: "1st Floor" had caused me to look for a multi-storey office block but there seemed to be no building higher than one storey. As I penetrated deeper into the maze-like bazaar, I passed a pool where the local ladies were beating their washing on stones and spreading it out to dry in the sun. I moved on along cobbled tracks accessible only to pedestrians or cyclists in the dry season and navigable by boat in the wet. I was now in the heart of a somewhat squalid bazaar, with its multitudes of tiny shops, most of them little more than a hole in the wall. The building which housed Trans-Orient Traders was certainly superior to these. It was about twenty-four feet square and the ground floor was given up to four shops, each about six feet in every direction, and selling a variety of useful articles from buckets to betel nuts. I walked round this edifice twice before I found the wooden steps leading to the first floor, which consisted of a storeroom and a ten foot by six-foot office – the home of Trans-Orient Traders. In line with the more austere outlook of industrial giants today, the office was simply furnished. it contained one rush-bottom chair, a small table with a battered portable typewriter, and on the red-splashed floor, a spittoon, obviously necessitated by the Proprietor's pan-chewing habits though recalling the ancient quip: "I miss the old spittoon." "Yes, so I see!"

    The room was empty and I left my card with a note suggesting that the Director should telephone me at my hotel.

He did not; he knew the game was up if anyone visited his establishment. He was one of the thousands of small "indenting-houses" who, for a few rupees, obtain tender specifications when they are published and try to obtain quotations and agencies from overseas suppliers.

Chapter 8 India

Calcutta

I was to arrive in Calcutta just before lunch, but the plane was an hour late. The Indian awaiting me had a programme for our four days together which was a model of planning. By omitting lunch, we could still make our first call on time, and work on through the afternoon. At 5.15 next morning I would leave, my hotel to catch the 6.00 a.m. flight to Jamshedpur, and since there was no return flight late enough the same day, he had made reservations for us on the overnight train, which would leave Jamshedpur at midnight and get us back to Calcutta at 7.00 a.m., in time for an early start on the day's appointments. The last day we were to leave by car for Durgapur at 7.00 a.m., with the probability of an early finish to the day, by eight or nine at night.

There are, of course, many ways of dealing with foreign visitors. You can sit them on a hard wooden chair and leave them all day while you continue with your normal work; you can provide a relay of young hosts to ensure that the guests never get to their beds before five in the morning. At one point in my itinerary where everyone had heavy colds, the method was to cough and sneeze over me until I either succumbed or left. Providing that he himself could stand the pace, the Indian's system would at least ensure that I never returned. But I wrong him; he had merely been asked by his Bombay office to make sure that my time was properly utilised.

The drive from Dum-Dum Airport, past the arsenal where the original dum-dum bullets were cast and on into the heart of Calcutta, is a staggering introduction to India and one which later visitors will miss when the new motorway is completed. Past tumbledown shanties, shacks and wayside stalls, we fought our way among a confused, shifting mass of cars, lorries, taxis, cycles, motor-scooters, men trotting in the shafts of rickshaws, carts pulled by men and carts pulled by oxen. Past men perched despondently on their parked rickshaws, in default of a fare, people washing in street hydrants, cooking by the roadside, sleeping on the pavements; a teaming mass of humanity in dirty white dhotis.

And it was hot! Policemen on point-duty in the city centre were shielded from the sun by white umbrellas, fixed in their belts to leave their hands free; pedestrians held newspapers over their heads to protect them as they walked.

Despite the full programme, I managed to visit the bookshop next to my hotel. In Karachi I had bought the second volume of a three-volume edition of Gibbon's "Decline & Fall", which, as an odd volume was ridiculously cheap. Here in Calcutta, I was unfortunately able to buy the first and third volumes - an addition of seven pounds to the luggage I had to cart around the globe. Bookshops are a source of temptation to me; as many men find themselves in bars, I am drawn into bookshops. Normally this is not a serious matter, but on a tour where I was limited to 44 lbs. luggage weight, it threatened to be calamitous. The airlines generously allow, in addition to the 44 lbs., "a reasonable amount of reading matter" for the flight. I wondered if this three-volume set, tucked under my arm, would be considered reasonable. I had already parcelled up a number of books and posted them by sea to my home and probably these would have to travel the same way. I once met a man who said that his "ambition" was to read Gibbon's "Decline & fall", and looking through my set, I now felt that his word was apt.

The hotel was being modernised and my rooms in the new section, but the servants were of the old traditional type. My "room-boy" was a gaunt, elderly Indian with staring eyes and a disconcerting trick of materialising soundlessly in the room. One morning I glanced in the bathroom mirror to see how I was looking, and saw instead a black face with staring eyes - he was standing in the bathroom doorway waiting to be noticed. My knees turned to water, my stomach inverted itself and I do not expect to survive this shock.

In spite of the usual ten per cent service charge, he wanted tips and I was quite willing to co-operate with him - it seems to be generally true that the service-charge is a concealed price increase and that tipping is still necessary, but I would have preferred some sort of arrangement with my "boy" where I paid to be left alone, since I find it inconvenient to be interrupted three times each hour to reconfirm that I have no more laundry, nor do I see why I should take off my shoes, so that they can be cleaned again, when I am on my way out. The hotel servants are always anxious to know how long you are staying and at first, in my innocence, I took this to be a friendly interest in my affairs. But the morning of my rising at half-past-four there was a panic and flurry among the "boys", because this usually indicates a departure by jet-plane for another country. Yesterday's Room-boy came in, today's boy followed hard on his heels and then the night-boy, with sundry porters and servants, all with a claim on my bounty.

At first I am sure they did not believe my story of a short visit to Jamshedpur, but felt that this was a mean and odious subterfuge to escape without paying. Not until they realised that I was taking only an overnight-case did they consent to leave me.

Jamshedpur

Jamshedpur is an hour's flight by Dakota. It is a town which has grown up around steel, engineering, locomotive and associated industries. Many of the factories here, as in other Parts of India, result from partnerships with foreign firms and are as modern and efficient as their counterparts anywhere in the world, but extreme shortage of foreign exchange creates many problems for them. An Indian gave me an interesting summary of the basic economic problems, some of which stem from the success of new industries which need materials from abroad but are not yet competitive enough to earn foreign exchange by exporting. He started this exposition by saying: "We Indians are a very sentimental people - over money!"

It had been a hot, dusty day and I spent the evening until departure time, at the small local hotel. I had taken a room there but was rather glad I would not have to sleep in it, and my colleague and I sat on the verandah, driven nearly distracted by the endless "ponk, ponk, ponk, ponk" of a bird in a tree on the other side of the road. By half-past-eleven, my friend and I had established ourselves in our two-berth sleeper. I had never travelled by overnight train before and had no standard of comparison, but this was a First Class, air-conditioned coach, and though the beds were hard, it was clean and comfortable. After a look at the bathroom at the end of the corridor I decided that I would prefer to stay dirty until I reached my hotel in the morning. My companion seemed to sleep well, but I dozed fitfully and with the dawn watched our progress through fields and villages ghostly in the waist-high mist. Howrah Station, Calcutta, in the early morning is squalid and depressing. It is not easy to get off the train for the Hordes of tip-hungry, red-jerseyed porters fighting to get at the luggage. One porter was stealing a march on his fellows by going in through a window head first. We emerged from the station, picking our way through recumbent Indians, sleeping wherever there was space to lie down. A short wait in a queue for a taxi and by half-past seven I was back in my hotel room. It seemed like home, and my gaunt, staring "boy" like an old friend.

Durgapur

We had hired a car for our journey to Durgapur, two days later. The driver had brought his brother-in-law and a friend, for company, but my colleague would not stand for this and the friend was discarded at a convenient point. Across the Ganges and out into the countryside we journeyed for eighty miles through dusty land, shimmering in the heat. We spent the day at Durgapur Steel Works and in the late afternoon set off, back to Calcutta. The heat was stifling; my colleague had dozed off; so too had the brother-in-law, and the car seemed to be going ever more slowly across the plain, but at first, I was not sure of this, as the speedometer was not functioning. Then I saw the driver's head pitch forward. He, too, was falling asleep and I leaned over, ready to take charge of the steering. Just at that moment, one of the tyres burst, and the bump and swerve woke the driver and our companions. The tyre was quite bald and in ten minutes they had replaced it with another, equally bald. Probably the extreme heat of the road was in part responsible, because a few miles further on, the spare tyre just fitted, also burst.

After my colleague had told the driver what he thought of him, he and his brother-in-law set off towards a village, trundling a wheel, while my friend and I waited and drank two bottles of lemonade which I had brought in my briefcase. Hot lemonade is not pleasant but helps to ward off dehydration.

It was dark before we were mobile again and the driver, in a furious temper, drove like a madman through the outskirts of Calcutta, among milling pedestrians, taxis, cars, carts, animals and rickshaws. Several times my friend told the driver to slow down, but he was beyond the reach of reason. Incredibly, we reached the hotel without accident. I was too late to get anything in the restaurant apart from tepid mulligatawny soup, followed by soggy rice and curried mutton, so-called, which was more probably part of the water-buffalo I had seen that morning on a cart, being pulled by the Indians it should have been pulling - the treacherous beast had died.

I wanted to post a letter and some cards but it was Saturday afternoon, there was no mail collection from the hotel until Monday and I decided to walk gently to the Post Office a few hundred yards away. Inside, I looked around to see where stamps were sold and was instantly taken under the protection of an Indian employee of the Office. I was glad of his help; posting a letter turned out to be unexpectedly complicated. First, he waited in line for a chance to weigh the letter, then reported this information at a counter where a clerk told him how much it would cost. After collecting money from me, he queued to buy the stamps and next took his turn to stick his finger into a dirty jar of dirtier glue, which he smeared over the envelope and cards as the stamps did not carry enough adhesive, and the "By Airmail" notices, none at all.

I was very glad I had not had to dip my finger in the gluepot and decided that I would give him a tip, in addition to the change from the stamp money, which I knew I would never see again. After waiting to have the mail franked, it was only necessary for him to post it, and the whole job was done, in considerably under an hour.

During the course of this tour, something like half a dozen letters failed to arrive at their destinations, but I was surprised that the number was not greater in view of the arrangements at many hotels. Often, guests' letters are handled by a shop in the hotel and the guest hands over the letter and money, without any guarantee that the one is ever applied to the other. Perhaps a strong-minded character might ask to see the stamps stuck on, but they can be removed and re-used by the attendant, rightly indignant at such an implied slur on his honesty and integrity.

New Delhi

From Calcutta we brought a plane-load of mosquitoes to New Delhi, though the ones straying within my reach were dead on arrival. The Indian passengers seemed unaware of this plague and looked uneasily in my direction as I grabbed spasmodically at the air around me.

Like the internal airlines of several countries, Indian Airlines provide "free-seating". This magic phrase, with all its happy connotations and associations, means only that they will not go to the trouble of allocating seats on a seating-plan, and that the passengers must race each other across the airfield unless, content to accept the least popular seats - the middle ones of sets of three. During the day, the aisle seats allow the bored traveller easy access to the main aisle where he can wander up and down, chat with the hostesses and beguile some of the monotonous minutes. On a long night flight, the window seat offers the hope of a little sleep. The man in the aisle seat has the two inner-passengers kicking his kneecaps as they periodically clamber over him, and has his shoulder and head banged and buffeted by passengers blundering along the darkened aisle.

I had not been prepared to queue for half an hour by the departure gate and was left behind in the race for "free-seating", so that I was the middle of three; on my right a gentleman who had apparently, as the start of a lifetime addiction, imbibed garlic with his mother's milk, and on my left an Indian lady with a large-eyed, bare-bottomed little boy on her lap. In the intervals of mosquito catching, I smiled and winked at him. He rewarded me eventually by jetting a bright arching stream over me. His mother hastily, if pointlessly carried him off to the toilets. Across the aisle, a small English boy stared at me and then, in a loud, clear voice announced: "Mummy! That man's wet himself!"

New Delhi, the seat of Government except during the hottest months, is a spacious and well-planned city with many fine buildings. It is also a convenient jumping-off point for many tourist attractions, including the most famous of them all the Taj Mahal. For me, unfortunately, through shortage of time, it was merely the jumping-off point for Bombay.

Bombay

I had intended to walk the few yards from the hotel to the "gateway to India" - a commemorative arch recalling the visit of George V and Queen Mary to India - but I gathered an entourage of tiny children, who would not go away even after the usual distribution of small change. One child was expertly patting my pockets to find out if there was more money in them, while another, more forthright still, had a hand burrowing into my trouser-pocket. I retreated, pursued to the doors of the hotel, refusing en-route offers to clean my shoes, change my money, or introduce me to some girls.

While admiring the Bay of Bombay from the lounge, I pondered the problem of the beggars, though without coming to any conclusion.

After a few days the most generous or wealthy person would realise the uselessness of indiscriminate charity, but it is difficult for a well-fed visitor to harden his heart. Leaving the hotel that morning with an American I had been shocked by a young man who was knocking on the taxi window with the stumps of his forearms. In a moment of revulsion, I thrust at him a rupee note which he nipped between his stumps and bore off, grinning with delight. The American told me that in one week, a compatriot of his had given away a hundred dollars.

"These people have so little," had been his excuse.

"But when you hand out money at that rate," said my companion, "you are tempting people to manufacture cripples, to cash in on their high earning ability."

Visitors from prosperous countries confronted by poverty and squalor, must at some stage hear the voice of their conscience, asking by what right they live so well. By an uneasy quibble I found myself glad that I was there on business and not for pleasure, although tourists bring urgently needed foreign exchange. The same illogical scruple prevented me, while I was in Calcutta, from taking a rickshaw for a short journey at rush-hour when no taxi was free.

I could not persuade myself to sit enthroned on a rickshaw, towed by a cadaverous barefoot Indian, sweat-rag in hand, trotting along on hot tarmac under a burning sun. If a rickshaw-man failed to eat, that evening, he was suffering for my principles.

And so, I walked. A young man fell into step and said: "You do not mind if a poor Indian boy speaks to you?" The sensible answer would be: "Yes!" - but it requires strength of mind beyond the normal to give it. As we walked, he told me that he was anxious to improve his knowledge of English; that he was saving up to become an engineer; that he was the sole support of a widowed mother and a family of brothers and sisters; that he strongly deplored the amount of begging that went on in India, and that he was always willing to accept a gift of a few rupees from a gentleman he had been privileged to guide back to his hotel. I could not resist a man to man approach of this sort and paid up. We then shook hands and parted with expressions of good will.

For religious and ethical reasons, India has a strong tendency towards abstinence from alcohol, although the position varies from State to State. In Calcutta there is one "dry" day each week; in New Delhi there appeared to be little restriction on drinks served to guests in hotel rooms, but in Bombay it is necessary for visitors from abroad to obtain a liquor licence.

This enables the holder to buy, at exorbitant prices, up to a bottle of spirits, or four bottles of wine, or twelve of beer, each week, and the main hotels have "Permit Rooms", open a few hours daily, where guests with permits may indulge their craving for alcohol. The Permit Rooms are very much like a normal cocktail lounge, but have a Police or Excise Officer on duty to ensure that the regulations are not broken without his knowledge. A good deal of form-filling is involved before a drink can he served and the final entry is on the visitor's permit to record the quantity of drink supplied each time and the cumulative total, rather like a bank statement except that there is no provision for overdrafts.

At one time, Indian residents of Maharashtra State could obtain a liquor permit against a doctor's certificate only, but there has been some relaxation and Indians over forty years old are now deemed to be capable of holding their drink like gentlemen and are granted permits.

Poona

It was necessary for me to visit Poona, a hundred miles or so from Bombay and I travelled there by rail.

The journey took about four hours but was well worth the discomfort of sitting for so long on hard, hot seats, as the line runs alongside the Western Ghats for much of the way, providing spectacular views of the fantastically eroded, corroded, etiolated and desiccated peaks which look like a moonscape. The final climb to Poona is through attractive mountain scenery, cool and pleasant after the humidity of Bombay.

Poona itself was a disappointment. This famous, hill-station figures in so many tales of British India and in the anecdotes of so many old army officers, that it was an anticlimax to find it a modern city, though still retaining links with its past. I think I must have been subconsciously under the impression that I was going on a tiger hunt.

On the return journey, the seats had become harder. Aldous Huxley, through a character in "Antic Hay" suggested trousers with an air-cushion seat so that those of us lacking the padding of the obese, could sit comfortably through long sermons, lectures and similar ordeals.

During my travels I had noted with tolerant amusement than most of my fellow-travellers seemed to be carrying with them enough pills, potions and tablets to stock a small shop. No doubt they had listened to the sort of advice I had decided to ignore, at the time I set out. When warned of the dangers of drinking the local water in foreign lands, I had said that so far as I was concerned, water was a liquid used for washing floors.

I reminded them of the old soldier asked about precautions observed in camp to ensure a safe water supply, who answered: "First we filters it, then we boils it, then we chlorinates it and finally we always drinks beer."

I had passed unscathed through five countries; in Pakistan where I had heard much of the "Karachi Trots" I had not even had to quicken my pace, but in Bombay I fell ill. I was assailed by cramp-like pains and my interior became a "cave of wind and waters". Progressively I reduced my diet until I was existing on a little boiled rice. I have always avoided pills and relied instead on a semi-mystical belief in the power of the body to throw off most ailments. Unfortunately, it had not recognised the urgency of this situation; I had now given up eating and was visibly losing flesh. Each morning as I confronted myself before the mirror, I saw deeper hollows in my cheeks and interesting new angularities, as the bone structure of my face asserted itself. I felt my nose -it was hot and dry; my eyes looked dull and reproachful.

Initially I had no doubt that my body could throw off this malady, unless I died of starvation first, but as the days dragged on, I began to lose faith, and I recalled the wretched weeks I had spent some years ago, while I was waiting for my body to cure me of back trouble. It had failed miserably, and I had finally been compelled to take the case out of its hands.

Curiously, I had just received a letter from a brother, advising me to take care of my back and my stomach, "for without back and stomach," he wrote, "what is a man? Nothing but an oversize wasp." At a happier time, I would have replied that even without back and stomach, a man could still have principles but after ten days of illness, I could no longer afford them, and on a Qantas flight I discussed myself with a friendly Australian steward. He gave me some tablets which started me on the road back to health, and I supplemented them at the first opportunity with bulk purchases of a variety of tablets to fix intestinal disorders - in fact, enough tablets to stock a small shop.

Bangalore

Outside the hotel in Bangalore sat an Indian snake-charmer, ready to put on his show for anyone emerging from the hotel on foot. He was imposingly robed and turbaned, and his eyes twinkled with good humour in his brown wrinkled face. Though old, he was probably younger and certainly fitter than his ancient, toothless cobra which swayed languidly to the wailing music. The liveliest member of the act was a young mongoose. The Indian was training it to attack the snake, but its baby jaws could not have grasped the cobra's neck and so the fakir was inciting the mongoose to attack the slender tail.

It was tackling this in fine style until the cobra, resenting the impertinence, turned and hissed fiercely in the mongoose's face, at which it leapt backwards three feet and scuttled behind the fakir.

The rest of the show included fire-eating, conjuring, posing for photographs, sale of souvenirs and a collection. I bought a snake-stone, which is a piece of wood the size of a florin, polished apart from a small section where the highly absorbent grain is exposed. If pressed on to a snake bite it will, said the fakir, extract the last traces of venom and he had letters from eminent surgeons in such places as Heidelberg and Belfast testifying to the value of these snake stones.

Bangalore, over 3,000 feet high, is pleasantly cool and peaceful after the heat and turmoil of Bombay. My room was not air-conditioned but had a fan mounted in the ceiling, near a large hook, conveniently placed for any guest wishing to hang himself. My bed was equipped with a mosquito-net which I shared both night's with a few mosquitoes. During the day I was taken to my appointments by a young Sikh, who drove as though at the wheel of a racing car. Slumped in a racing crouch, with his head tied up in a turban and beard like a pudding ready for the pot, he hurled the car about in fine style. Because of this, I spent my time clinging to fixtures to avoid being thrown around the car and was too preoccupied to see much of the city.

I was intrigued, however, by the number of wild monkeys to be seen even within the city and could not rid myself of a feeling that someone would shortly round them all up and put them back in cages.

Madras

From Bangalore I moved on to Madras, the third largest city of India and a major port. Hotels were unusually full because; the New Zealand Test cricketers were there and I was unable to get an air-conditioned room. That night, after sweating until 1.0 a.m., I abandoned the hope of sleeping and wrote letters and reports until seven, finishing tired but with paper work up to date.

In Madras too, I encountered the engaging South Indian habit of shaking the head in token of affirmation, approval and strong agreement. It is not quite like the British shake of negation, though near enough to create confusion; it is more of a lateral rocking of the head, which I found captivating and am cultivating personally.

Here also, I met gentlemen with names like Ananthanarayanan, Balusubramanyam and Rajagopalachari - the longest names in my experience, though shortly to be eclipsed by a Mr. Soerjanatemihardja in Indonesia

CHAPTER 9 Burma

The Burmese are a friendly people with little of the British desire for privacy. At present, however, by decree of the Revolutionary Government, Burma is working out its own path to Socialism, free from contaminating western influences. Tourists are not wanted, despite the valuable foreign exchange they could provide and it is very difficult to obtain a visa for anything longer than a 24-hour transit stop.

At the Strand Hotel, Rangoon, a "boy" showed me up to my room while two more took my suitcase and briefcase. All four of us entered and then the Room-boy arrived, and to show who really belonged there, started adjusting curtains, fiddling with the air-conditioner and re-making the bed. Meanwhile, attracted by the crowd, two barefoot Burmans in khaki shorts and shirts -the lowest echelon of servant - who had been pretending to sweep the corridor, wandered in and stood gazing around with obvious interest. I wondered if I could slip out unobserved, but apart from the khaki-clad boys with rush whisks, who were there from friendly curiosity only, the other four unless tipped would have remained there indefinitely. Because of the absence of tourists there are too many servants chasing too few tips.

The other hotel for foreigners is the large Inya Lake Hotel, a few miles out of the city. It was completed several years ago and was by way of being a gift from the U.S.S.R., following a visit of Khrushchev and Bulganin. As I heard the story, all the Burmese had to provide was the site, the materials and the labour. Probably fewer than a dozen guests were in residence and that evening I dined alone in a splendid banquet room with elaborate chandeliers brilliantly illuminating the scene. I felt:

"Like one who treads alone,
Some banquet-hall   deserted;
'Whose guests are fled,
whose garlands dead,
And all but he departed."

But by the time I had reached the cheese course, two more diners had arrived and with my coffee, a third. I left then; I hate crowds.

Inya Lake itself is beautiful, even in the rainy season. Its highly irregular shape, with inlets, creeks, bays and islands - gives it the appearance of greater size - it is not quite three miles long. Its English name is Victoria Lake but this is dropping out of use. A map in the Rangoon Sailing Club shows features of the lake with such evocative names as "Isle of Wight", "The Needles" and "North West Passage". Sailing on Lake Inya is as pleasant a way of spending an afternoon as may be imagined.

The Pagodas look like giant, gilded handbells. The largest, Shwedagon, is a few miles out; Sule Pagoda is right in the centre of Rangoon, completely encircled by roads as though on a large traffic-island and with many small shops clustered round its base. Wandering across the roads, at the hazard of their lives, go little old ladies, carrying umbrellas and smoking Burma cheroots. The streets are littered with cigar stubs just as with cigarette ends, in England.

There are few private businesses left; the mammoth People's Stores Corporation is responsible for the distribution of almost every commodity in Burma. After the fashion of large organisations, it is somewhat cumbersome and in general there is little evidence of administrative efficiency or of a rising standard of living. Walking in Rangoon can be risky unless you keep your eyes on the ground, as the pavements are undermined by legions of busy rats, and in the rainy season, the paving stones give way, tilt, or splash a gallon of muddy water over your feet. If you walk, you must accept an escort of taxis and cycle-rickshaws who cannot believe that you seriously intend to walk - clearly it is a low, British trick, to beat down their price. Even if you are crazy enough to walk in the Turkish bath atmosphere, you must want to change dollars illegally, and up to three times the official rate is offered. However, on entering Burma, all forms of money must be declared and all currency-exchanges recorded on a form to be returned to Customs when departing. This does not stop illegal deals but it makes them harder.

At the "Strand" were a few tourists passing through on 24-hour transit-visas. One who did not sleep at the hotel was a young student - let us call him Paul - who had solved the problem of how to travel without money. On the ride from the Airport, when I assumed he would be staying at the hotel, he said, "No, I sleep at the Sikh Temple!" Charity, he explained in his excellent English, is a religious duty of the Sikhs and he frequently obliged them by providing a worthy object.

Buddhists too, could be relied on for a night's free lodging, but he found them too eager for a religious argument. He wanted to sleep. Failing either, he would often sleep at Airline offices, or when in funds at a Salvation Army or Y.M.C.A. hostel. He was now heading back home ready for the new University term. When compelled to buy tickets he obtained them at students' concessionary rates; on occasion he had "thumbed" lifts from private or military aircraft. He had enough money to get as far as Kuwait, he considered, and there he would sell some of his blood for about twenty dollars. There was an apologetic note in his voice at this point; he was not proud of anything as honest as this — if he could have sold someone else's blood, or fooled the blood — bank with diluted ketchup, he would have felt happier. In India, Pakistan and Ceylon he had transacted illegal currency deals; he had driven by car from Europe into South India and illegally sold the car, adding bribery and corruption of officials to his crimes.

In Ceylon he had solved the problem of how to turn illegally obtained rupees back into dollars by locating someone who would forge entries on his currency form; he had bought a number of Swiss watches into India and sold them at three times their cost; he had — as the tale of his iniquities grew, there seemed only one omission:

"Haven't you overlooked dope smuggling?" I enquired.

He laughed. "It would be easy, but I do not do it. These other things, if I am caught, I am just a stupid young student and they kick my backside and send me home — but drugs, no!"

Business in Burma seemed to involve mysterious meetings after dark with go-betweens, undercover workers, contact-men and others, all with the same proud belief that there is no situation, however unpromising, that will not produce a profit to skilful operators.

There is a patriotic emphasis on "Burmanisation" which perhaps accounted for the notice in the morning paper that "Blossom Ho will henceforth be known as Ma Aye Aye Myint." Attractive though the latter name undoubtedly is, if I had the good fortune to be named Blossom Ho, nothing would induce me to change it.

Chapter 10 Bangkok

"How long you here for?" enquired the duskily attractive Thai waitress.

"Just a few days". "You are alone?" "Yes", I admitted.

."What is your room number?"

"Seventy-six", I said. In fact, I was not staying at that hotel - merely having coffee there, but she had omitted to ask that question.

As I left the air-conditioned comfort of the hotel and emerged into the enervating, steamy heat outside, a dark figure approached.

"You buy ticket - 'blue' movie?"

"No thank you," I answered politely, and climbed into a taxi.

The driver handed me a grubby card. It read:

"This driver will take you where there are thirty pretty girls wishing to be of service to you."

I was flattered - thirty is a lot of girls for someone of my age and temperament, but I gave him the name of my hotel instead.

In Bangkok it is desirable to select a taxi-driver who is small and frail, since you will have to have an argument with him at the end of the journey. Taxis are of the conventional four-wheel saloon type, or a little three-wheel two-stroke vehicle normally avoided by foreigners, unless weary of life.

All taxis have meters; in no taxi does the meter work. Guide-books advise the traveller to negotiate the fare in advance, but fail to explain how this is possible, firstly without causing a traffic-jam and secondly when you have no idea how far it is to your destination, nor what is the local scale of charges.

On arrival, the taxi-driver may give you a quick glance, or will stare directly ahead as he says; "Twenty-five Baht" -or, "Forty Baht" - usually about four times the true charge. If you are a good actor and can either burst into peals of laughter or put on a show of anger, it will help.

"I give you ten Baht - and that's too much!" Eventually it should be possible to settle for no more than double the correct fare.

Traffic is chaotically congested in Bangkok, and motor horns blare endlessly. It would be more convenient for the Bangkok drivers if the horn wiring were reversed so that it was necessary to press the horn button to stop it blowing.

At the Airline office, I had just reconfirmed the next stage of my flight. I had done this in several countries now and was learning some new telephone-alphabets, as the clerks spelt out my name over the telephone. This time, the initials of my first names were given as Roger Foxtrot which I thought an attractive alternative. This system of clarification explains why I was once welcomed by someone expecting to meet a Mr. Charley Alice.

As we entered, the appropriate strains of the "Ride of the Valkyries" filled the room, to be followed by a Beethoven Sonata for Violin and Piano, and by works of Mozart and Handel. I commented on this choice of background music to one of the two Vikings (the first I had seen in horn-rimmed spectacles) and he said:
"WE like it!"
The popularity of their restaurant suggests that their customers either like it too, or do not object to it. So far as I was concerned, I realised at last the reason for a vague sense of disappointment after the many orchestral concerts I had attended over the years - they had forgotten the food!
Unfortunately, my companion insisted that we move on to a night-club. Entry to Bangkok night-clubs involves only the purchase of a drink - they are not really clubs. We visited a succession of these, confirming me in a private view that even hardened drinkers find it a boring occupation, and must hope to infuse some element of interest by the "crawl" from one to another, every half-hour. This "crawl" took us on a descending path with each club more sordid and seedier than the preceding one. My companion was becoming noisy and I was becoming apprehensive. The last call was at a bar displaying a notice reading:
"The girls in this establishment are on their own and not connected with the Club in any fashion. The Management refuses to be held responsible in any way for their behaviour or actions."

I had stopped drinking about five clubs previously, and cold sober - watched my companion start to pick a quarrel with a drunk. It was almost three in the morning and the place was still full - There were the "girls", the dregs of the streets, still-unattached at this hour, listlessly drinking and watching a number of male couples dancing. I tried to make myself inconspicuous behind two glasses of beer I was not drinking, and wondered if my children's lives would be seriously affected by the belief that their: father had been knifed in a drunken brawl in a "dive" in Bangkok. By suggesting that we try another night-club, I persuaded my companion to leave, and once in the street I put him in one taxi and myself in another.

Two, days later he took me around the, Buddhist temples and down the, river and canals. The temples are called "a photographer's paradise" and are certainly impressive, though I felt as I had in Rangoon that for Western eyes there is, perhaps, too much gold-leaf used. The river and the canals leading from it are flanked with dwellings. Thai infants bob around in the stream like corks; the older boys attach themselves to passing boats and take a free tow for a few miles, casting loose when they have had enough, or see the chance of a tow back again.

Friendly Thai housewives stand in the stream washing their hair or their clothes or their babies, and watching the passing boatloads of tourists.

This is the world of the river; they live "by it and with it and on it and in it". The Thai riverside dweller could say with Rat of "The Mind in the Willows":

"It's brother and sister to me, and aunts, and company, and food and drink, and (naturally) washing. It's my world and I don't want any other."

My journeyings had taken me through parts of the East where visiting Western concert artists were rare. Thai classical ballet and Madras dancing were well enough, but I found myself hungering for familiar music. Wherever I went I seemed to be either too late or too soon for some celebrity. I was too late for Campoli; too early for Kendall Taylor, but in Djakarta sometime later, in the ballroom of the Hotel Indonesia, I attended a recital by a German pianist. This rare treat attracted not only a capacity audience, but, high up in the lofty room, a delegation of cicadas who showed their appreciation by chirruping shrilly, so that we had Beethoven's Moonlight and Appassionata Sonatas, for Piano and Cicada. The louder the music, the louder they sang. It was a memorable recital by a novel combination, not without its possibilities.

In Bangkok - though this has nothing to do with music - I bought a couple of harmonicas with the vague idea that my sons would like them, although I think I knew well enough what would happen to them.

After some practice in the privacy of hotel rooms I had made limited progress. The main difficulty was to find tunes without sharps or flats, which slowly, but tunefully went up and down the scale. There seemed a real shortage of these. "God Save our Gracious Queen" presented no problems, but I felt that to play it in some parts of this region of the world might be considered a deliberate, neo-colonialist provocation, and I always played it very softly, with an apprehensive eye to the windows.

"Drink to me only" was my next achievement, followed a, night later by "Waltzing Matilda". Then I hit a bad patch, when I could neither play anything new, not even this small repertoire which I had acquired so laboriously. No doubt I had overdone the practicing - I have heard other artists speak of the same problem. After an hour in which I appeared to be playing "God Save Matilda" and "Drink to our Waltzing Queen", I abandoned the instrument in disgust.

"Why don't we see a movie?" suggested the American with whom I was sitting in the hotel bar. This, of course, is the danger of making casual contacts - the weaker partner finds himself taken over. However, I was at a loose end and not in a mood for working in my room. The cinema sounded a better idea than sitting for several hours in a bar. Perhaps "The Last Time I saw Paris" would have reached Bangkok by camel-back from Lahore.

The ordinary Asian presumably knows no more of the Western world than gleaned from the movies, television and the behaviour of white tourists, which is a frightening thought. In the hotel lounge I had noted with interest American programmes on the T.V. set, with speech dubbed into Thai. Synchronomously with this (as Mr. Polly might have said) the original soundtrack is also broadcast by a radio channel so that Westerners can turn down the sound on their T.V. sets and watch the vision while picking up the English soundtrack from their transistor radios. All this ingenuity so that the races of the world may share "Batman".

We found ourselves in a taxi and my companion handed a card to the driver.

"What are we seeing?" I asked.

"Something real good! A boy outside the hotel gave me that ticket."

"Just a minute! Do you mean 'blue' movies?"

"Why sure! You didn't think I was meaning for us to see 'Mary Poppins', did you?"

I subsided and resumed my normal state of readiness for an instant sideways evacuation of the taxi when one of the driver's hair-raising manoeuvres proved to have failed. No doubt I would survive a 'blue' movie - it would certainly be an improvement on "The Last Time I saw Paris". My companion was an old Bangkok hand having arrived there two days before I did.

"Say," he continued, "have you been to one of these massage parlours yet?"

"No", I confessed.

"Boy, oh boy! This you must not miss!" he exclaimed extravagantly. "Dusky maidens powdering you all over and singing little Thai songs to you!"

I was not impressed; no-one has powdered me all over since my infancy and I believe I can still recall the panic which afflicts the ticklish in these circumstances.

Our taxi had fought its way through the sprawling, centreless chaos of Bangkok and stopped at a doorway near one of the innumerable night-clubs. We ascended a flight of stairs and for the sum of one hundred Baht (five dollars) each we were admitted to a large room containing twenty or thirty seats and a dozen or so Westerners - including two women and three Thais. Music from a tape-recorder was presumably intended to keep the audience happy and there.

After five minutes another white male came in - followed within seconds by two uniformed Thai policemen, revolvers at hips and, even at this time of night, wearing the inevitable sunglasses which appear to be as much a part of their uniforms as the peaked hat.

"Place stay seated everybody", said the senior man while his assistant remained by the door.

Speaking in adequate English the police officer told us that we were breaking the laws of his country in coming to see obscene movies.

His instructions were to take names and addresses, nationalities and passport details from all foreigners present. No one would be able to leave Bangkok until his Department had decided whether or not to prosecute. Our party now looked like a tableau of Consternation for a modern morality play.

"Say Bud - Sir", pleaded my colleague, "I have to be in Hong Kong Friday".

The policeman shrugged.

"You know", broke in an English voice, "we are not watching obscene movies."

"We have just seized the movies and projector below", said the policeman. "Perhaps you can explain for what reason you are here?"

There was silence. Then the policeman said, "You know, you are foolish peoples. How if I come to your country and break your laws? But here we like tourists and do not wish to embarrass you. Perhaps I let you go this time - only foreigners please - and do not be foolish peoples again!"

I led the race to the door, closely followed by other very white faces and leaving only the impassive three Thais. There was no tendency to talk and no one loitered to ask for his money back. All frantically hailed taxis and made off into the night. In the melee on the stairs my companion and I had become separated and I did not see him until late that evening when he hailed me into the bar where he was drinking with another American.

"Wow!" he exclaimed. "Was I a worried boy a few hours back?"

He started to explain to his new friend what had befallen us. He listened with extreme interest, merely punctuating the story with, "The Hell!", "The Hell you did!" and "The Hell you say!" Then, unaccountably he slapped himself and laughed long and noisily. Exactly the same thing had happened to him two nights previously. Police had entered just as he was seated and waiting for the "blue" movie show. After lecturing the "foolish peoples", the police had allowed them to go, holding only the three Thai members of the audience and the doorman. Again no one had bothered asking for their money back. Clearly a few enterprising Thais had hit on an ingenious way of relieving tourists of surplus dollars. No "blue" movies were required, no screen or projector — just two accomplices dressed as Thai policemen.

Chapter 11 Saigon

I spent my first evening in Saigon having a haircut. I had nothing in mind other than the usual "short back and sides", but the barber did not make the mistake of asking for instructions. He made a workmanlike, if lengthy job of the haircut and without a break moved straight into the profitable part of the sequence.

I was massaged manually with chopping strokes from the edge of his hands and then with a devilish electric vibratory device, which set my teeth chattering, my cheeks shuddering and my chins buzzing - face, scalp, head, shoulders - nothing escaped. Then he twisted my ears till they cracked, tweaked my cheeks, realigned my eyeballs, poured half a pint of fluid into my hair and kneaded vigorously. Finally he pulled my head back to an angle which prevented me from swallowing, and cooked me under hot towels while I filled up with saliva.

    Staggering to my feet, I asked him how much I owed him for all this, and, with a bland Oriental smile he indicated the back of the room, where a beautiful girl was seated at a desk. This was smart; who would haggle with her? She gave me a ticket reading 350 which I paid, and a further hundred to the barber, now brushing imaginary hairs from me - a total of about thirty shillings, but it had been an interesting evening, cheap at the price.

    My hotel had a good name; rather superior in sound and associations to, say, the Waldorf-Astoria, but it had nothing else to recommend it. I was there only because despite a firm reservation, the Continental Palace Hotel was full when I arrived and passed me on to this establishment, one of the many which have sprung up to cash in on the desperate shortage of hotel accommodation.

It was just a few rooms up a winding staircase. Though in theory air-conditioned, my room was like an oven because there was no electricity. By loading air-conditioners on to an inadequate circuit, in which fuses had been replaced by copper wire, some costly damage had been done. The water supply failed during the first day and thereafter one or other of the two boys running the hotel brought up water in a bucket.

I lay naked and sweating through the night. Planes droned out on operations and soon gunfire and bomb explosions rattled the windows. Towards dawn it became cooler and I dozed long enough for the mosquitoes to close in. Soon I was awake, scratching frantically at a hundred bites. Though I have never yet been to prison, the room reminded me of a cell in its bare drabness and I wished I could remember what crime I had committed. The following day, during the siesta hour, despite the heat of my room I lay down, hoping to sleep, but the slam of a door and the raised voice of the occupant of the cell below, quickly dispelled that idea.

It was an American soldier on Rest and Recreation leave after combat duties. He had been drinking and had some grievance against one of the two Vietnamese youths in charge of the hotel.

"Don't give me any of your lip, you sarcastic son-of-¬a-bitch," bellowed this gallant ally of South Viet-Nam. "I don't want any goddam lip from you. I'm a free-born citizen of the U.S.A. and my name is Lewis B------- not Hu Flung Dung.

I told you to do it and why the hell didn't you? Why? Why? Why?- Why? Are you stoopid or what?"

The boy's voice was too soft for me to hear his reply, but after Lew had told him, four times more, that he was a free-born citizen of the U.S.A., I retired to sleep in one of the armchairs in the lounge of the Caravelle Hotel, nearby.

That evening, after a late dinner at l'Amiral Restaurant, I returned to my hotel. The small alcove, about twelve feet square, at the head of the first flight of stairs, served as an office, a lounge and as a bedroom for the two Vietnamese youths. A Ship's Engineer who introduced himself as Bob, was playing Brahms' Lullaby on a harmonica so small that his capacious lips sometimes engulfed it. As a fellow-artist on this instrument, I applauded him, fetched my own harmonica and we exchanged repertoires. We were joined by a young Negro soldier and harmonicas were interchanged in a spirit of unhygienic bonhomie. The Ship's Engineer specialised in vibrato effects; the Negro in syncopated rhythms, and together they produced some lively music for me and for the two Viet boys, who were stretched out, one on the desk, the other on tomorrow's sheets and towels, attempting to sleep through all this. The towels, incidentally, bore all the signs of having been dried but not washed, which made me slightly unhappy. If I have to have a dried, unwashed towel, I would prefer it to be my own.

There was a noisy altercation at the foot of the stairs, by the entrance from the street. The free-born American citizen, Lew, had arrived the worse for drink and in the care of a Negro Military Policeman, who, with a white colleague was engaged in clearing the streets of stragglers, still out after the midnight curfew. Lew had decided to resist, and had just called the Negro M.P. a "dark-faced son-of-a-bitch". Sternly, the Sergeant pushed him with the flat of his hand and Lew fell back in a sitting position on the stairs.

"Don't hit me, Sergeant!" cried Lew, the craven no longer even pot-valiant, "I didn't mean anything, Sergeant!"

This must have been one of the quickest promotions on record; from "Dark-faced son-of-a-bitch" to "Sergeant", in two seconds.

"Hit you!" said the Negro Sergeant contemptuously, "Man, I'm trying to help you:"

Lew was escorted into our midst by an even drunker soldier who had just arrived back and who, after swaying to and fro for a few moments announced that he was "tahd" and going to bed. Meanwhile, the young Negro soldier had put down my harmonica and, shaking his head sorrowfully, but with an air of calm reason, confronted Lew.

"You shouldn't have 'called' that Sergeant on account of his skin," he said.

Lew denied that he had, and as an afterthought added that he was a free-born American citizen. The Negro repeated the charge and appealed to the Vietnamese youth now sitting up on the pile of towels. He looked uncomprehending as, in fact, he was.

"You want to go in for that sort of stuff back in the States - that's your prerogative," continued the Negro, maintaining with some effort his attitude of calm reason -"but as long as we're here, don't go 'calling' a man for his colour."

"I don't know why the hell we ARE here," shouted Lew. "All I want is to get back to civilization and never goddam leave it again."

"Well and I don't reckon we should be here either, but there's no cause for 'calling' a man on account of his colour."

"I never said a goddam thing about colour," yelled Lew.

"You telling me I didn't hear it?" said the Negro, all pretence of calm gone. Lew moved across the room for no apparent reason.

"Don't brush me out of your way!" said the Negro.

"Now you're picking on him," interposed the Ship's Engineer, "can't you see he's drunk?" The Negro ignored this. Moving across to Lew he said:

"Why don't you 'call' me for my colour?" He was trying to provoke Lew into calling him a "dark-faced son-of-a-bitch", so that he would have an excuse for killing him, but Lew was not drunk enough for that. This seemed a good point at which to leave the party and so I picked up my harmonica and sneaked quietly away.

The following day, after still another night without sleep, I managed, mainly through the influence of a friend, to get myself transferred to the Caravelle Hotel. When leaving my original hotel, I presented the young Negro with a harmonica. For some vague reason, I felt out of sympathy with Lew, despite the fact that he was a free-born American citizen.

I had looked forward to the opportunity of practising my French while in Saigon, since it is still the second language here, though rapidly giving place to American English. Certainly, after a few days I was speaking English with a strong French accent, but in general, by the time I had worked out, not what I wanted to say, but what I could say - the conversation had moved two topics further away from me. In one restaurant which I had been advised to try for its French cuisine, I realised that I had just ordered nightingales instead of kidneys, but it did not matter since they had neither.

This was one day when I was lunching alone, and the waiter stood by while I tried to select from over a hundred items. Kidneys, I gathered, were off; so was chicken; so too were steaks.

At this point, I put down the menu and asked what was "on". Only "saucisse" and "haricots" - there had been an accident in the kitchen - a fire! I refrained from asking him why on earth he had not told me this, without letting me waste time over the menu. My restraint was partly due to my inability to translate this instantly into French, which had a steadying effect, like counting ten before bawling someone out. I accepted the sausages and beans and was rewarded for my forbearance by seeing a party of six businessmen going through the same performance, a few minutes later. Someone was being "entertained", and, after the usual style of business lunches, it took five people to look after one visitor.

There was a good deal of joking, chatter, and exchanging of ideas as they went through the menu, the waiter meanwhile looking-on benignly. When they had all settled on what they would like, the head of the party - the man who would eventually push the bill across to his assistant - started to give the order. The waiter was sorry. Oh! too bad! Well, let's see now - why don't we have? Three times the waiter allowed this to happen before he disclosed that only sausages and beans were available. Surprisingly, no-one hit him. In silence they rose and left.

In Saigon, too many people are chasing too few taxis -a classic inflationary situation, leading to higher fares and to the use of substitutes, such as motorised rickshaws in which the passenger reclines in a basketwork contraption - acting as the driver's first cushion against a crash. Because of the passenger's forward position, he projects well into the stream of traffic before the driver can see if it is safe to proceed, and sudden braking would probably pitch the passenger into the path of whatever the driver wanted to avoid.

Any youth with a Lambretta-type scooter plies for hire, and in desperation I perched myself on the rear seat of one. The boy drove slowly around the centre of Saigon, shouting to his friends to find out if they knew the street and hotel I had named. Then he speeded up, apparently determined to cover every street until I recognised the one I wanted. It started to rain and we slid on clay from the many road-workings, amid the roar and confusion of the Saigon traffic. After what I guessed to be eight miles travelling, I recognised my hotel and paid off my driver, making a mental vow never to treat life so lightly again.

The next day, having obtained a street-map, I was able to walk the journey - it was less than half a mile direct, and took me past the Roman Catholic Cathedral with its graceful statue of the Virgin Mary. In Latin, on the pedestal, it says: "Queen of Peace, pray for us."

Barbed wire - a feature and symbol of Saigon today - is wound round the base, providing equally barbed comment, if more were needed.

Because the Caravelle could not fit me in more than two nights, I ended my stay in yet another hotel. This is memorable firstly because of an American businessman with whom I was discussing the U.S.A.'s immense material wealth. He said:

"Yes, you guys really ought to blackball George VIII or Henry VIII or whoever it was lost you your American colonies. He sure cost you a lot of dough."

Secondly, as I was passing the Reception Desk, one of the clerks started to tell me how desperately short of rooms they were - even to the extent that they had a problem over a very good friend of the Manager, who was arriving that day, and "would I, as a personal favour, let him share my room?"

"No! Certainly not: I don't share my room with anyone."

"He is a very nice gentleman - very clean - a friend of the Manager!"

"Then let him share the Manager's room."

"But the Manager sleeps with his wife!"

I would have liked to say: "So?", or "Then put a cot in their room," but contented myself with repeating that no-one was sharing my room.

CHAPTER 12 Manila

To escape from the unseen occupant of the next room, who had kept up a tuneless whistling throughout this Saturday evening, I had descended to the Hotel Lobby where a lift attendant was spitting into one of the ornate, brass, sand-filled ashtrays. My letter writing there was interrupted by a Filipino youth who introduced both himself and his Scandinavian friend to me. The Filipino had apparently lived a crowded and interesting life, which included four years at Sydney University, seven years in Honolulu, ten in New York and a boyhood in Manila. Either he was older than he looked, or his arithmetic was faulty. He was fluent in Japanese, having lived in Tokyo several years, he told me, his chromium-edged teeth flashing as he chattered.

Fortunately, he then left with his dour, lanky Scandinavian friend, who was departing from the Airport towards midnight. They made a strangely assorted pair.

The following morning at nine, my 'phone rang. It was the Filipino:

"You remember our interesting talk last night, sir, about my knowledge of Japanese?" "Oh, yes!" I said.

"I thought I might come to your room and talk about your country, with you."

"Oh, no!" I said. "I'm just on my way down."

As I waited for the lift, I suddenly wondered how he knew my room number. But, of course! My key had been at my side, on a piece of perspex almost long enough to use as a walking-stick, designed to prevent forgetful guests from leaving with their room-keys. Considerable thought has been applied to this problem. A straight length is not the complete answer because it can be slipped into a trouser-pocket, and providing the occupant of the trousers does not sit down, he may overlook it. One hotel attaches the key to a large cross, like the arms of a kite, hammered crudely from angle-iron. Another variant is the key on a ball and chain, which would tear its way through a pocket and smash the guest's toes. Old ladies may be seen staggering under this burden until relieved of it by a courteous male guest.

However, although the young Filipino must have seen my room-number as the key lay at my side, I was certainly not happy about the fact that he had memorised it. He was sitting facing the lift. I went to get a newspaper and decided that as a polite gesture, I would let him talk for five minutes and then leave him. He actually lasted less than a minute. The conversation went like this:

"I took my friend to the Airport. I had taken him around Manila because sometimes I work for tourist bureau, because I am only one who speak Japanese."

"Oh, yes?"

"I am very glad to see you again. I thought a lot about you since last evening," - he turned to look me soulfully in the eyes, - "in fact I dreamt about you!"

I departed hastily; the Whistler was preferable. Between the Whistler and the poor air-conditioning, I had spent two bad nights and I asked the Front-Desk to send someone to look at the air-conditioner, as it did not seem right that I should lie sweating through the night. The man who came put his hand in front of the current of air and asserted that all was in order. I denied it.

"Moving air always feels cooler than stationery air", I said. "This contraption is just a fan and a humidifier; the cooling part doesn't work."

We parted amicably but without having reached agreement, and so I had myself transferred to another room. The air-conditioner was just the same, but at least I had got rid of the Whistler, and as I started to tackle the air-conditioner with my pen-knife, I found myself whistling happily. The principle of the thing seemed clear enough. A device like the radiator of a car, received cold water from a central point outside, supplying all rooms. Air from my room was drawn past the radiator, cooled by it, and blown out from the top of the apparatus. The warmed water inside the radiator returned through external pipes to the central plant outside, which replaced it with cooled water.

I found that the radiator had become so choked with dust that the air was by-passing it and therefore no cooling was taking place. I worked busily for an hour, grimy and sweating, but cool air was now blowing into the room. As I replaced the covers, there was a crackle and a blue flash. I had allowed the thermostat to short-circuit against a metal panel.

The air-conditioner was now silent, and so was I as I completed the reassembly of the apparatus. Now it was really hot in the room. I wondered what the Hotel's reaction would be if I had to say that, oddly enough, the air-conditioner in this room was not working. A thought occurred to me and I switched on a reading-lamp. No light: Of course - just a fuse! After taking a shower I rang for the room-boy.

"The lights in here don't work," I said, "I think the fuse must have gone."

Within minutes, lights and air-conditioner were working and I looked forward to a good night's sleep - the first for three nights.

Although tired, I stayed up until midnight because of the slamming and banging of doors which takes place until most of the guests have either gone to bed or gone out. After I have been dragged back from the borderland of sleep half a dozen times within an hour, I lose the ability to fall asleep. But shortly after midnight I was fast asleep and soon after three I was wide awake, brought back unwillingly and unhappily to consciousness by a salvo of door-slamming from my new neighbours.

I tried to pretend that I was not really awake and that I was not quivering with rage, since in this pretence lay my only hope of resuming my sleep. But then their radio was turned on and the party came to life. It was a noisy party; there seemed to be five or six present, and they had undoubtedly drunk plenty before their return to the hotel. There was a lot of squealing from the girls, and some rearrangement of beds and furniture was taking place.

A complaint by 'phone to the Front-Desk produced no improvement and so I dressed and went down to do battle - with the Front-Desk boy. I did not feel called upon to tackle half a dozen noisy drunks in a city where the carrying of guns, coshes and daggers is far too prevalent.

"What," I asked, "is going on? How many people are occupying that room?"

"Only two, sir," he said, "I expect they have guests".

"Guests.' At three in the morning! What sort of establishment is this? Now will you please get that party wound up and the guests returned to the streets so that I can sleep".

I went into the all-night cafe and drank tea and read until I felt sleepy again. But there was no more sleep for me that night. True, they had turned down the radio slightly and were a little more restrained, but this meant only that I was having to listen more intently. At six in the morning, no doubt feeling that the night was over, they turned the radio up again.

The Management obligingly transferred me to yet another room. It was an interesting fact that each room was better than the previous one, which suggests that it pays to complain. If I had stayed a little longer, I could undoubtedly have worked my way up to the Presidential Suite.

An American, long resident in Manila, had been detailed to look after me and assumed that I would want to make a round of night-clubs and strip-joints. I declined with thanks. On this tour I had already been taken to one strip show which was staged behind locked doors for a private audience and I considered that my education was completed. As a form of entertainment, it seemed very limited and I could have summed up my attitude by paraphrasing a remark of Dr. Johnson's: "Sir, when you have seen one naked woman, you have seen all naked women - let us go to hear Kendall Taylor." For I had caught up with this famous pianist and I invited my American friend to join me at the recital that evening. I could not persuade him; all his life, he had understood that "long-haired" music, as he described it, was not for him, and that this was something to be profoundly thankful for. His early conditioning had saved him from the need to listen to any "long-haired" music and make up his own mind.

Later, when he was sharing coffee with me in my room, I gave him a short harmonica recital consisting of "My Old Kentucky Home" - which goes well on this plaintive instrument - and the "Ode to Joy" theme from Beethoven's "Choral" Symphony.

I played this twice without alarming him by naming it, and he said: "Gee! That's catchy - what is it?" I told him and congratulated him on joining the "long-haired" ranks. This was a trifle underhand but we were on friendly terms by then, and this small blow was struck not against one sort of music or for another, but against the "tyranny of the closed mind".

During the day he helped me find the disused theatre where tickets were on sale. For a moment I wondered if the ticket buying was designed as a test to eliminate all who were not really keen to attend the recital, for we sweated our way twice around the building before we found a little anonymous door leading up rickety stairs to an office where at last I bought my ticket.

The recital itself was held in the very attractive Philamlife Auditorium, cool, clean, and decorated with friezes of the spirited wood-carvings for which the Philippines are renowned. It was a fine setting in which to hear a great pianist play a programme which he had obviously selected with me in mind.

With a Dutchman from my hotel, whom I had met during the interval, I walked back - a walk punctuated-by taxis pulling up to offer us "Blue" movies and the range of night attractions which have made Manila notorious. In the hotel, he retired to his room and I to the Coffee Shop for tea. This hotel's idea of making tea was to dip a tea-bag into warm water, but I was educating them to the idea that for me, it had to be boiling water.

Kendall Taylor arrived, dress-coat over his arm, with a small group of his recital organisers. I could have told them that they had taken the wrong table. They had entered during a quiet minute while the juke-box drew breath. Now, at Kendall Taylor, fresh from his communion with Beethoven, Bach, Schubert and Scarlatti, the juke-box brayed forth obscenely.

On the pianist's impassive face, no sign of suffering appeared. "'A very gallant gentleman,'" I muttered as I escaped from the bedlam.

Smuggling is a major industry of the Philippines, and posters are displayed appealing to the public to shun it, as harmful to the Nation's economy and integrity. Local cigarette manufacturers, grinding a private axe, ask smokers not to purchase smuggled American brands, but to buy the local makes, which are as cheap, though apparently less popular. It is, of course, very difficult to prevent smuggling in a nation composed of thirty million people, inhabiting over seven thousand islands.

Manila is a modern, Western city, located in the Orient. Despite four centuries of Spanish rule, relics of this period are surprisingly few, though the names, appearance and religion of the people provide ample evidence.

The mossy ruins of Fort Santiago and the old city walls convey an air of slightly melancholy peace. An ant hill from which the ants have gone, is a dusty horror; a deserted beehive looks tragic and futile, but cities are improved by the departure of their makers, though always bearing scars.

The guide-books make special mention of Manila Bay which, to be blunt about it, is just a bay, and months later when showing colour-slides to a captive audience, I had some difficulty in distinguishing between Singapore Harbour, Manila and Bombay, nor so far as the audience was concerned did it seem necessary.

CHAPTER 13 Taiwan

"Why, hallo there:" It was clearly the surprised but delighted cry of an old friend from England, amazed to see me in Taiwan. I paused and turned. A Chinese shopkeeper was closing up on me rapidly.

"Now don't go away," he begged, "I want the pleasure of showing you round my shop."

How he had assessed me as British I am not certain - possibly because I needed a haircut. If I had had a crew-cut no doubt he would have hailed: "Why, hi there.' Shopkeepers of the Orient have many talents, though some still drive away potential business by pestering anyone who even glances at their window or slows his pace.

At the Great Eastern Hotel in Calcutta, for instance, the hotel shops, or "tourist traps" as they are generally called, are on each side of a narrow corridor leading to the breakfast room. The proprietor lurks within until - perhaps alerted by vibrations - he scurries out like a Trap-door spider from its hole, and tries to drag the victim in. Further along, another shopkeeper stands obliquely, partially blocking the corridor, and attempts to divert the flow of tourists into his shop, as water into an irrigation channel. Yet another waves his arms, talks volubly, and tries to bustle the tourists in, as though corralling cattle.

Taiwan drives on the right of the road, nominally. There is the usual frantic driving and the normal pointless blaring of the horn. Few taxi drivers speak English. After a visit to the town centre I took a taxi and asked for the President Hotel. "Pre-si-dent?" queried the driver.

"President," I confirmed. He wrote something in Chinese and passed it to me. I passed it back.

"President," I said, again. "Like Chiang Kai Shek," I added.

He thought for a moment and said, "King?"

This seemed a reasonable translation from someone knowing no English, of the functions of a President, so I agreed and he set off madly, pulling up ten minutes later outside the Ambassador Hotel.

Taipei engages in a flourishing business of pirate-publishing a wide range of literature and technical books. I had been told about this in Manila and thought it deserved investigation. True enough; I was appalled to be able to buy a volume of short stories by Maupassant, Dreiser's "Sister Carrie", Mann's "The Magic Mountain" and "The Making of a Quagmire" - a recent book on Vietnam by Halberstam - each at about half the published price. The first two were "Modern Library" editions, but in the copying process the name of the publisher and series had been omitted. All four books are now located in my bookcase as clear proof that this nefarious trade does in fact take place.

The whole of "Encyclopaedia Britannica", Toynbee's "A Study of History", the "Shorter Oxford" and "Chambers'" Dictionaries, many technical works, standard classics and the latest fiction were there, again at about half price. In every instance I checked, the paper seemed heavier and glossier, and the binding more substantial though less attractively finished than the originals.

Taiwan was formerly known as Formosa - the Beautiful Isle, but it earns this title rather from the exotic mountain scenery, than by its capital, Taipei, which is not remarkable for beauty. During my short stay I scarcely saw the sun; low cloud and rain persisted depressingly. The dreary weather meant at least that I was content to spend a weekend working. There are two extremes to be avoided as I had already discovered.

To compile sections of a general report on a country before completing the visit, usually involves rewriting them, since on the last day or in the last hour, some new information or fresh development alters the way the report is "slanted" and its conclusions. On the other hand, to delay writing reports on a tour of this sort may mean that impressions of one country are overlaid by those of two or more countries subsequently visited, and a conversation with a Commercial Officer which actually took place in Calcutta is, through a mental lapse, allowed to colour a report on conditions in Burma.

My final meal before leaving for Hong Kong was a pleasant and well-organised lunch with one of the Taipei Rotary Clubs. For the closing ceremony of singing the Chinese National Anthem, I was provided with a card giving the Chinese words in English characters together with an English translation. The tune gave me no trouble; I know now that my voice is better suited to the East since the wailing cadences and general effect (to Western ears) of off-key flatness come naturally to me.

Chapter 14 Hong Kong

Perhaps it was partly the sunshine that made the difference, but there were also other advantages which made my stay in Hong Kong seem like a holiday interlude. Its tax-free, duty-free status draws hordes of tourists from all over the world, lusting after bargains but often proclaiming their innocence by the phrase: "Is that American dollars or Hong Kong?" With a rate of 5.65 H.K. Dollars to one U.S. Dollar, they should hardly need to ask, and have certainly damaged their bargaining position by indicating to the Chinese shopkeeper that they do not know, to within 500% or so, the price of the article. This large tourist traffic means that Hong Kong has the best hotels in the region and I now understand fully why so many newspaper articles on China or Indonesia or Vietnam, come from "our correspondent in Hong Kong". I stayed at the Peninsular Hotel in Kowloon on the mainland, a ferry-ride from Hong Kong island - and rated it the best of all the hotels I used during my world tour, because it offered luxury with dignity rather than with ostentation and achieved a certain "period" flavour refreshing to the spirits after the noisy brashness of so many modern hotels.

The Crown Colony of Hong Kong consists of Hong Kong Island, the peninsular of Kowloon and the New Territories - leased for 99 years in 1898.

The prosperity of the Colony and the small area available have forced builders high up the mountain sides, and multi-storey buildings are fantastically perched where it would seem impossible for a mountain goat to gain access or foothold. A spectacular view of this, by daylight or night is obtained by a ride up the Peak Railway.

The Island looks tiny when viewed from a 'plane, but a drive round by car corrects this impression to some extent. A popular ride is to Aberdeen, where I was ferried to the Tai Pak Floating Restaurant and enjoyed the best Chinese food I have tasted anywhere. "All unconscious of their doom" the fishy materials of the meals swim around in a pound at the side of the Floating Restaurant until selected by a diner who, after pronouncing the death sentence goes inside and waits for his victim to be served up. I recalled a hotel on the A.I. in Yorkshire where, years ago I was invited to select trout from the graceful speckled creatures swimming in a tank. At that time, I was not completely sullied by "the world's slow stain" and I refused, to the surprise of my companion, a Yorkshire man, who said that "brass" alone signified in this part of England and that for a price the Hotel Manager would unquestionably be willing to strangle and serve up the pet canary then singing energetically in its cage.

Tai Pak Restaurant displays pictures of some of the Royal personages, film-stars and other celebrities who have eaten there.

On leaving, I was given a pair of chopsticks, one of which I shall have sharpened at the point so that food can be speared; the other can be drilled vertically for use as a drinking-straw. This is the only way I can ever hope to take a meal with the sole aid of chopsticks.

Hong Kong has a special importance to the Press as (in their phrase) - a "listening-post" to find out what is going on in China. The dedicated newsmen may be found hard at work, listening until the early hours of the morning if need be. Certainly, the noise in some of the bars is so great that unless someone were listening hard, the Red Guard could march in unheard. This concept of the "listening-post" is perhaps the most significant discovery of modern times. Formerly, a reporter wanting to know what was happening in Peking, or Djakarta, or Hug, would go there at considerable personal inconvenience, put up with poor hotels and bad food, and confuse himself with a lot of facts, often very irritating to his employer. Now, free from this sort of bias, he can listen in comfort and keep his mind on the important business of reporting what his readers want to hear.

Whatever Hong Kong's value as a "listening-post" there is no doubt about its importance as a trading post for China and through it comes a wide variety of products - from fans and carvings for the tourists, or china and clothing for the home, to lifting-tackle and machine tools for the factory - usually at staggeringly low prices, since China wants foreign exchange. American tourists must obtain a certificate of origin to prove that the Chinese souvenirs they are buying were not made in China, and the infinitely obliging Hong Kong shopkeeper finds this no problem.

In Hong Kong and Kowloon there are two department stores selling only goods from "Red" China, and I spent an hour or so one evening looking round. Because of the weight problem I restricted my buying to a sandalwood fan, three traditional Chinese scenes painted on silk, and a jade ring. Ahead of me at the jewelry counter was an American also buying a jade ring which he explained would fit his wife's finger, providing it would just pass over the top joint of his own little finger.

 I guess I'm going to have a little Customs problem when I get back - we don't deal with Communist China."

We discussed the difficulty and decided that anything controversial is best kept in the left-hand jacket pocket so that it can quickly be produced when asking for the guidance of the Customs officers. We further agreed that it is very easy to forget odd items in the left-hand pocket, and that one rarely hears of ordinary travellers being searched by the Customs officials.

Chapter 15 Seoul

My five days in Seoul, the capital of South Korea, left no striking impressions. Probably I was reaching the stage of confusion of an Australian Prime Minister on a quick tour of the Far East, who said, at a banquet in Seoul, how glad he was to be in Taipei. The interpreter corrected the slip and it was left to one of the Prime Minister's fellow-countrymen to put it on record.

In Seoul, everyone with whom I talked business appeared to be named Kim, except the American head of a local distributor company. Apart from the accent, I would have assumed him to be British, though I do not mean to suggest or imply that this was creditable in him. At dinner one evening in his pleasant home, he outraged his wife's sensibilities by stating that the vegetables we were then enjoying were fertilized with human excrement, and hoping I did not object.

It was in Seoul too that an American guest at the same hotel invited me to his room "for a whisky" and then gave me Bourbon in Coca-cola. At such times it is depressingly obvious to me that no permanent British - U.S.A. alliance is possible.

South Korea seemed to have in circulation the dirtiest money I had seen, in a region of dirty money. The Roman who said: Petunia non olet - (money doesn't smell) was of course speaking figuratively.

As in other countries of the region, notes are doing the work of coins, owing to inflation. Among my wad of notes were some of value one Won - less than half a Cent.

Chapter 16 Tokyo

Although I had no business to transact in Tokyo, a kindly company apparently felt that I had earned a few days break and had made arrangements with associates there, to look after me. And so, as I emerged from Customs at Tokyo Airport, I saw two smiling Japanese holding a small placard bearing my name and a leaflet of one of my Company's fork-lift trucks. With typical Japanese thoroughness, they had ensured that even if I could not read my own name, there was a picture to attract my attention.

It was Friday evening, and I was feeling jaded and weary. On the flight I had eaten too soon after a farewell lunch in Seoul, and was regretting it. My general intention was to have a quiet evening and retire to bed early. On the drive from the airport to the Okura Hotel I discovered that my hosts were planning to entertain me that same evening, rather than the following night as I had expected.

This is one of the problems and hazards of short visits to countries. Business etiquette and reciprocal courtesy will normally necessitate several dinners out, and late nights which neither party particularly wants. Earlier, I had visited four countries in rapid succession and had not had an evening to myself for ten days.

I showered and changed while my hosts waited in my room. The younger man, whom I judged to be about twenty, had no English and was restricted to smiling. His colleague was probably in his mid-thirties and spoke English adequately for our limited purposes.

We dined Japanese style, on Sukiyaki, so appetising that I forgot my indigestion, washed down with saki which made me forget that I was jaded.

Following the meal, we drove around the Ginza before visiting a night-club. It was the best I visited during my travels -reasonably quiet, properly lighted and decently conducted. My host had obtained four hostesses, Japanese in Western dress. Though perhaps a trifle extravagant, it meant that each male had a hostess on either side. However, only one spoke English and so my two hosts entertained three of the hostesses while I entertained the English-speaking girl. She was relieved to learn that I cannot dance and - which should follow logically but rarely does - do not attempt to.

She was free to rest and practice her English. She seemed a charming and intelligent girl, and probably was, but several drinks of Suntory whisky after the earlier saki, had created in me a general sense of well-being, not specially conducive to the exercise of the critical faculty. None of our party was dancing; all were content to relax with a drink and conversation.

Sometime between midnight and one o'clock I discovered that my host lived sixty miles out of Tokyo, was going home that night and would be returning the following morning to collect me and to look in at his office. I insisted that I was tired and we prepared to go. On the way out, I saw a man I recognised. He hailed me and I moved over to his table. It was the American I had last seen buying a ring in Hong Kong, to take back to his wife. The coincidence was not great; I had already become accustomed to the fact that foreigners in Asia tend to visit the same cities, use the same few hotels and frequent the same tourist spots.

He had an attractive hostess at his side and was holding her hand.

"I got the answer to that problem about the ring." he exclaimed, grinning broadly.

"Problem?" I said.

"You know - getting stuff from Red China past Customs back home. It's not going home. It's staying right here! She likes it and she's going to be very grateful. Isn't that so?"

He raised her hand for me to inspect. There were several rings on her fingers, but the one she tilted towards me and which she was herself admiring with the pride and satisfaction of new ownership, was the jade ring.

Chapter 17 UFO'S

Racing the sun across the heavens at an altitude of 33,000 feet gave us a twilight and sunset lasting about an hour and a half. The sunset was of a splendour I had never seen from the earth, and to have this extended threefold was awesome. A little nearer the Pole or a little faster, and time would have stood still for us.

By my side was an American scientist who attributed the spectacular auroral effects to volcanic dust and said that these high-altitude sunsets had been at their most impressive some eighteen months previously. He commented acidly on our fellow passengers.

"A sunset like this and no-one watching it! You'd think everyone would be fighting for places at the windows but instead they've brought paperbacks to kill time. I tell you, aircraft designers might as well stop putting in windows - just give them a T.V. screen and the "Flintstones".

He also spoke harshly of the modern willingness to believe that "everything is possible", which understandably set his scientific teeth on edge.

"The man in the street", he said, "loves to think he's smarter than his ancestors; that all the time new knowledge is overturning the old and that what they believed has been proved wrong. There is no new knowledge," he cried with a sweeping gesture that just missed my tea - "Newton is not proved wrong by Einstein and all things are not possible!"

As an instance of the public's gullibility, he spoke of Unidentified Flying Objects. He referred to a newspaper report of a scientist - here he looked as though he might be sick - supposed to have seen a U.F.O. and on the assumption that it held beings from outer-space, to have flashed his car's headlights at it, three times, once, and then four times. The flashing of 314, the approximate value of pi, was intended as a message to indicate to the U.F.O. that intelligent creatures inhabit the earth.

"Now, what a farrago of nonsense to publish!" exclaimed the scientist contemptuously. "Only because we have ten digits and therefore a decimal system, does 3.14 represent pi. Suppose these creatures from Space had seven digits or used a binary system - either of which would be better than the decimal system what then? But this is the sort of pseudo-scientific garbage the public loves!

With a snort of disgust, he picked up his Agatha Christie paperback and settled down to read.

My own paperback contained an amusing story of men, captured and in cages on another planet, who try to solve this same problem of proving their intelligence, by weaving baskets from their bedding material, whereon their captors decide that this is an instinctive courtship ritual and put a woman from another cage in with them.

Chapter 18 Singapore

In Singapore I had the use of a flat, the home of a business acquaintance whom I had twice met in England. He was on home-leave and the flat was in the care of his elderly Chinese housekeeper who had her own quarters adjacent to the flat. The Amah's English was negligible and her accent puzzling but she showed great ingenuity in doing without language. After she had retired to her own flat towards nine each evening, I would help myself to cold drinks from the wide assortment in the refrigerator. In a few days I discovered her system which was simply to provide at first an assortment of drinks and a variety of Chinese and European foods, rather like scattering bait on the water to see what the fish are taking. As soon as she had discovered my preferences, she confined her catering to these.

Later, I was able to ask the Chinese secretary at the office of my Company to telephone the flat to explain anything I had not managed to convey to the Amah.

As they spoke different dialects of Chinese, they used Malay as the common factor.

From a weighing-machine I learned that in my longstanding battle to keep flesh on my bones, I had lost ground to the extent of another pound and a half. Taking a sheet of graph paper, I plotted my weight over recent years and projected it into the future. By 1984, at the present rate of loss, I shall weigh only five stones and by the year 2000, I shall be back to my birth-weight of ten pounds. By April 7th, 2024 when I shall be a hundred years old, I shall weigh nothing at all. Like the "Incredible Shrinking Man" I shall have faded completely away.

It was Sunday, and we lay around the swimming pool at a friend's hotel, basking in the sun. Nothing much had happened for over three hours apart from periodic visits of the waiter to replenish glasses and an occasional swim in the pool by one of the more energetic members of the party. An Australian, resident in Singapore was there with his wife and after the conversation had centred on Saigon for some minutes, she said:

"Saigon? Saigon? ... let me see - isn't that the place where they've had some trouble lately?"

She knew she had heard of it somewhere!

As we lazed, there was a general agreement that for good living and good eating, Singapore was one of the jewels of the East.

"I had a devil of a job keeping my Director away from, here," said one of the party, taking his pipe from his mouth. "But for fifteen years I made it, although he was always saying that he must come and get a first-hand idea of our operations here. Fortunately, the newspapers 'play up' every trifle and I managed to convince him what a terrible place this was to live and work. Why, they felt sorry for me, back at Head Office!" he exclaimed. "I used to send them cuttings about any odd riot and once I got myself photographed in an armoured car and sent them the picture. Then too, I used to splash items all over my expense claims for things like prickly-heat ointment and jabs against yellow-fever, black-water fever, cholera, typhus, bubonic plague - the lot! Not that I had the jabs," he added. "Just the ones you've got to have when you go to other God-forsaken countries. But it really impressed them. They thought I was a dedicated Company man. When he got here finally, my Director said: 'This isn't a bit like I expected!' and I said: 'No, well it's improved a lot in recent years'".

There was a general laugh. Most of the white residents of Singapore live in luxury, with servants and a standard of living which few of them could afford in their home countries.

Even for the native Chinese and Malays making up the bulk of Singapore's population, living standards are far higher than in almost any other part of Asia, which makes it a pleasant country to visit. White residents sometimes complain of the sameness of a climate where everything - temperature, humidity and rainfall - always seems to be in the eighties. The highest point of the island is Mount Faber, which is 470 feet high, and "from its summit" as one of the guide-books says, "a panoramic view of the island can be obtained." Some of the beaches, with palms almost at the water's edge, achieve a graceful charm, but after a short while the flatness of the terrain leaves only an impression of unrelieved and tropically profuse vegetation, recalling the comment of the painter who said that Nature is "too green, and badly lighted."

When I was nine, I was given for Christmas a book of eight hundred jokes. A family legend grew up over the ensuing years, that I had memorised the book of jokes and that they were my unvarying stock. While this was a slander, I had certainly become conscious of the need for a new audience, and at last, a mere 8,000 miles from home, I found one in the person of the demure Chinese secretary who was working for me.

Not merely the immortal eight-hundred, but also the worn-out quips of yester-year were new to her, and for the first time in decades I shone, sparkled and scintillated like a newly polished diamond.

"A gentleman always raises his hat before kicking a lady", I had said, not expecting any reaction other than the gloomy silence of a family determined, in my own interests, not to encourage me. But she laughed! It was new to her; perhaps she thought it was original, and as I realised that they were all new to her, out they came for a frolic in the sun.

I was invited to her home and finding a family of seven daughters, could not resist commenting that at school we had been told that the Chinese wanted sons, and daughters were looked on as misfortunes to be drowned at birth. Quite clearly I had been misinformed. All spoke good English, with a slightly literary flavour to it, as well as Malay and Hokkien. A very young-looking mother organised a banquet of Chinese and Malay dishes, in honour of the grandmother, an elderly lady with a wide and warming smile, who presided over this family gathering. The father of the girls seemed quite cheerful amid this feminine avalanche.

The races indigenous to this region of the world are exceptionally attractive, or rather, they seem to produce a higher proportion of attractive specimens, both male and female, than equivalent groups of white people. This was made apparent to me by the behaviour of a young English fellow in his mid-twenties, just out to join a British Company for three years, who was constantly requiring to be pulled back from under the traffic because his eyes and attention were following the girls passing by.

If anyone of them had taken the trouble to walk right round him, unquestionably his neck would have been broken, just as an owl's can be wrung by anyone who walks round it three times.

He was already, in his own view, an expert in the haggling by which prices are established. He indicated his sunglasses, a famous German make, and told me how he had beaten down the seller in Change Alley, from 27 Straits Dollars (about £3) to 7. Before we had gone another hundred yards, one of the lenses fell out and smashed on the pavement, revealing one very surprised eye. He complained to the local agents of the famous German firm, who were able to prove that it was a cheap, illegal copy. A much more impressive bargain was the Omega watch he bought in the street a few days later for about £4. When it had gained two hours a day in the first couple of days, he went to an authorised Omega dealer, though why, I am not sure, since it had a tick like an alarm clock and a winder-ratchet audible at fifty yards. No, it was not an Omega and had never been! Genuine Omega watches are hard to find at £4.

Also in and around Change Alley are the money-changers, mainly Indian, who, with lightning rapidity will cover a notepad with calculations which mean nothing - the important figure work goes on in their heads. If you bargain hard and shrewdly, you can often get nearly as good a rate for your dollars or pounds as at the adjacent Bank.

Change Alley is a low, narrow, little tunnel, flanked with little stalls and shops and roofed with toys and other merchandise. If you do not faint from the heat, you will merge into Raffles Place, where there is a new underground car-park, and on the far side, a fixed-price department-store for those who do not enjoy haggling. This involves sitting patiently in the shop while the assistant plies you with Coca-cola - a shrewd stroke since you will be reluctant to leave without buying something, after accepting free drinks and also must accept the price after a reasonable time, or explode. For the residents, haggling becomes an almost automatic process, and an English lady described how, after years in Singapore, she horrified a shopkeeper in her native Woking by suddenly going into the haggler's patter of, "Oh, no! That's far too much; I wouldn't dream of giving that for it!"

All around are shops and arcades stuffed with tax-free, duty-free cameras, radios, amplifiers, record-players and tape-recorders, representing an unbearable temptation to visitors from other countries, and even for local residents. I met an Indian engineer who admitted to owning four tape-recorders and about twelve cameras.

"A friend of mine," he said, "considers that I must have been deprived of toys when I was a child!"

Chapter 19 Malaysia

Penang

The Fokker "Friendship" called at Malacca, Kuala Lumpur and Ipoh on its way to Penang, and our obliging hostess offered sweets for each take-off and landing - a total of eight-mints as well as sundry sandwiches and cups of tea. This was my third breakfast, since, after a light meal before leaving the flat at six that morning, I had spent the waiting time at Singapore Airport in the snack-bar, mainly to enjoy its upholstered seats instead of the wooden benches in the departure area.

The "Friendship" flew at about 15,000 feet altitude and though suffering more turbulence than the high-flying jets, it did provide a spectacular view of Malaya's wooded mountains and of the pale green and brown scars of the tin mines. I had assumed that a tin mine, like a coal mine, would be a shaft drilled vertically down into the ground, but here, tin mining is a dredging and washing process, leaving pools and sandy areas which stand out vividly against the prevailing carpet of dark, luxuriant green.

It was lunchtime when we landed at Penang and I was entertained to an Indian meal in which I identified curried goat and giant fresh-water prawns as thick as my wrist.

Penang is a popular holiday island with many fine beaches and with sea breezes to temper the tropical heat. In George Town, the capital, the two best known hotels provide a complete contrast in styles, since the Eastern and Oriental is in the old tradition, and is one of a number in the East said to have been mentioned in Somerset Maugham's stories, while the Ambassador has only recently opened and offers smartness and sophistication.

Kaula Lumpur

In Kuala Lumpur, the Federal capital, I spent a day with a Chinese salesman, allegedly speaking English. I hasten to add that I am certainly not presuming to criticise his English, which was considerably better than my Malay. In addition to these two languages, he spoke Thai and Cantonese, but he had thrown me badly for a start by telling me that he used to sell "weakles". After querying it twice, I had to pretend that I knew what he meant and had, in fact, been no mean "weakle" salesman myself. The mystery was not cleared until after lunch, when he said "motor-weakles", and by then I had another problem to solve because he said:
"Afternoon, we visit Jinnah's factory."
"Jinnah?"
"Yes — Jinnah's factory."

Jinnah, as the founder of Pakistan, I had heard of, but Jinnah in Malaysia? And with a factory? Surely this could not be right. On the way he referred to it again, this time as "the factory of Jinnah's Towt" — and sure enough, within minutes we had pulled up by a signboard saying: "Guinness Stout."

The following day I drove to Port Dickson, past plantations of rubber trees, weeping latex tears into cups strapped to their trunks, past plantations of oil Palms and through the most dense and luxuriant vegetation I had seen. In addition to oil refineries, Port Dickson has a beautiful beach fringed with palm trees, and a motel offering:

"Meals in the garden, with the birds to keep you company." Perhaps 'birds' is used colloquially, because the introductory message continues:

"The motel is quiet, select and discreet ... You can enjoy a weekend or a longer stay."

CHAPTER 20 Djakarta

In the early stages of my tour, as a fledgling member of the "jet-set", each take-off and each touch-down had been an event for which I had mentally composed myself.

Until the pilot indicated, by retracting the undercarriage, that he at least, considered us airborne, I would not start reading. Similarly, at the end of the flight, when the cabin-indicators instructed passengers to fasten seat-belts, and as the hostess announced the local time, the temperature on the ground, and so on, then I would close my book and turn my mind to solemn matters; the hopelessness of our position if one of the engines, glowing redly in the night, were to fall off; the tragedy of my young life cut short; my widow and my fatherless children. However, it soon occurred to me that since I could do nothing, it was pointless thinking about a possible crash; that my young life was purely subjective, and that in view of the amount of life-insurance cover provided by a generous company, I was showing a mean, selfish spirit by clinging so tenaciously to life.

Familiarity had hardened me to the extent that, deeply absorbed in a book, I was frequently unaware of the take-off, but I noticed a tendency to ensure that I had finished any alcoholic drink, and that the evidence had been removed, before we reached the critical point of descent.

On thinking about this, it seemed that although regarding myself as a devout agnostic since the early age of eight (when the failure of prayer was revealed to me by the continued presence of one of my teachers) - nevertheless it was obvious that part of my mind believed in a Creator, and had no wish to appear before him, slurring words and giving other indications of Partial-drunkenness. First impressions are important!

My standards were finally eroded by the nonchalance of long-service international men. Some regarded the 'plane as an extension of their offices and were deep in paper-work as soon as they took their seats. A few reminded me of Jerome K. Jerome's friend (a hearty eater) who chose the all-in rate for a week's cruise. Rough weather upset his stomach and calculations. At the end of a week during which he had lived a "simple and blameless existence on thin Captain's biscuits and soda-water", he watched the ship departing and said:

"There she goes with two pounds' worth of food that belongs to me and that I haven't had."

So it is with the First-Class passenger on an International Airline. Apart from extra space, and a few frivolities such as bedsocks, the only economic gain is free drink. Some passengers were clearly determined to emerge on the credit side of the bargain by drinking more than the (substantial) difference between First, and Tourist Class fare.

With these dedicated men alongside me, my modest drinking habits would surely pass without comment in the event that the whole 'planeload of us made an untimely appearance before the Almighty.

There was no one to meet me at Kemajoran Airport, Djakarta. Although I had cabled arrival details to the local agent, the cable was not delivered until later. Normally, the local agent is happy to extend this courtesy and normally I was happy to accept, though to be met by a deputation of men with several years accumulation of problems and grievances, at midnight (their time) - three in the morning (your time), after a seven hour flight, is not relaxing.

But the man with local knowledge can often sort out minor problems and speed the visitor through the entry formalities. His familiarity with local currency regulations can also help. In Burma, for example, I had changed too many Traveller's Cheques into kyats, and later discovered that I could neither reconvert the surplus into another currency, nor take it out of the country. On my final full day, after paying the hotel bill and allowing sufficient cash for taxi, airport dues, breakfast and tips, I used the balance of Burmese currency to buy Cassell's French Dictionary (weight 21 pounds) from the Strand Hotel's bookstall, and a box of cheroots.

Even so, at the Airport next, morning, I still had the equivalent of ten shillings in kyats and to avoid the crime of taking it out of the country, presented it to a lavatory attendant - the only Burman I could see around, apart from Customs and Airline officials. It occurred to me later, that this might have been open to misinterpretation, but at six in the morning I am not clear-headed, particularly when I have not slept. The formalities of departure can extend backwards through a dreary night. When I left Djakarta the timetable was:

    6.00 a.m.   Take-off. (This has to be treated seriously despite an inner-certainty that you will be lucky to be away by 7.00).

    4.30 a.m. Check-in time. (The normal one-hour for international flights was here extended to one-and-a-half hours).

    4.00 a.m. (Allow half-a-hour for taxi journey from hotel to airport).

    3.30 a.m. (Allow half-an-hour for bill-paying at the hotel, for assembling luggage and for securing a taxi).

    2.30 a.m. (Allow one hour to drink tea and reconstitute my personality).

    Accordingly, I retired to bed at 11.00p.m. the previous night and lay wakeful through the usual hotel barrage of door slamming, eventually lapsing into a coma about 12.30, from which I was awakened at 1.00 a.m. by my telephone.

The Reception Desk wanted to know whether I intended leaving by the airport 'bus because if so, I had better hurry. I did not have the spirit left to be rude to them even though they knew, and I knew they knew that I was not using the airport 'bus - because they handled the taxi reservation for me. By 2.00 a.m. I was dressed, packed and ready for a flight which eventually departed at half-past seven.

The local agent caught up with me later in the day in my room at the Hotel Indonesia. He hoped that I would be free to dine with his boss but regretted that he himself would not be present since it was now the month of Ramadan, when Moslems fast each day from sunrise to sunset. His boss, he explained, though also a Mohammedan, had an ulcer and was excused fasting, on medical grounds.

At dinner that evening I expressed sympathy to my host, while we were tackling a full-scale Chinese meal, following a light snack of frogs' legs, which he had ordered, by way of a compliment to me, under the impression that they were a typically British delicacy. None of this I would have thought suitable for an ulcer sufferer, but perhaps a refusal to admit limitations helps. Courageously too, he refrained from looking like an ulcer-victim. He was plump, gay and carefree, with bright eyes twinkling behind his glasses, and teeth flashing in a perpetual broad grin. Later he referred to himself as a "statistical Moslem - one who helps to make up the numbers" and I privately judged him to be a statistical Moslem with a tactical ulcer.

Djakarta is famous, or notorious for its network of canals, engineered by the Dutch, which now serve every conceivable function for the poor of the city while exposing them to the gaze, indifferent, disgusted, curious or despairing, of the passer-by.

Within sight of these unfortunates, are the prestige building projects which Sukarno hoped would help in the task of creating a nation and a sense of national pride. Most are unfinished and work on them is halted, but Sarinah, Indonesia's first Department-Store, was opened prior to the fall of Sukarno, and the young of Djakarta, newly introduced to escalators, spend their days riding them. Inside the store are many Japanese and Russian products such as cameras, radios and fans, all at prices far beyond the reach of the ordinary citizen.

The streets of Djakarta were a maze of pot-holes and puddles - partly due to the rains but aggravated by neglect. Through the streets crawled a congested stream of cars, usually ancient and rarely modern - often broken down but bowling along briskly from the efforts of half-a-dozen Indonesians trotting behind. The ordinary citizen's transport is the tricycle-betjak which Sukarno planned to replace by motorised betjaks on the grounds that the former involved degrading labour for the man pedalling along in the sweltering heat. Sukarno has gone but the betjaks remain, with a few motorised models here and there.

I enjoyed a drive to the mountains through countryside of beauty and charm, past rice-paddies, rubber-estates, tea plantations and on into the mountains, cool and refreshing to the body and spirit after the heat and squalor of Djakarta. We passed through the town of Bogor containing the Presidential Palace where, in his days of power Sukarno "gloried and drank deep". It is a fine, white building set in attractive grounds. Raffles of Singapore was once Lt. Governor of Java, and his wife died at Bogor. A temple in the Palace grounds is dedicated to her and she is also commemorated by a quatrain which Raffles wrote:

"Oh thou whom ne'er my constant heart,
One moment hath forgot;
Though fate severe hath bid us part,
Yet still - forget me not."

CHAPTER 21 Perth

When setting out on a long car drive, a friend of mine used to make himself comfortable by loosening his shoe laces and unbuttoning the waistband of his trousers, until, getting out of the car one day in a hurry, his shoes fell off and his trousers dropped down. Nevertheless, the principle is sound, and the experienced traveller devotes time and thought to his comfort.

"In the old days," said an American at my side, "the hostesses had time to do a good job. "First", he elaborated, "you would get a hot towel as soon as you were in your seat, then candy for take-off, later a drink, magazines, food, cold towels and so on. But flight times have been better than halved and the girls have to keep running to make out."

"And supersonic flight is on the way," I contributed.

"Yeah! I guess then they'll have the cabin crew all lined up ready, and as you climb the steps to the aircraft, one girl will pop a candy in your mouth, the next will hand you a cut-lunch, the third give you a quick wipe with a hot towel, and so on. Mind you," he continued, "service is pretty lousy on some lines right now. The other day I saw a hostess shaking a guy who was asleep by the shoulders, and saying: 'Do you wanna magazine? Do you wan "something to read?"

At this moment, the Captain's very English voice announced that during our flight over the Indian Ocean we had lost our hydraulic oil, and the undercarriage would have to be lowered manually. I closed my eyes and feigned sleep, in case volunteers were required out on the wing for this operation.

"This is standard procedure," he continued imperturbably. But British captains always sound unflurried, and would doubtless announce that the plane was regrettably just out of fuel, in the same calm manner, whereas, though providing excellent service, Japan Air Lines usually manage to sound sinister or ominous, as the voice from the P.A. system speaks of "your fright-crew", expresses the hope that you have "enjoyed your fright", and the wish to "fry with you again."

The landing at Perth, Australia involved nothing more, alarming than fast braking and a wait on the landing strip for a tractor to tow us in. Perth Airport in the early hours has a ghostly air, due no doubt to the traveller's awareness of his utter remoteness. He is perched on the western tip of a vast country consisting it is said, of "five cities in a desert".

The nearest of these is almost as far away as Moscow from London, but between Perth and Adelaide is little but scrub and desert. Of the five cities, one is built around possibly the most beautiful harbour in the world, and two of the others would take high places on many travellers' lists of attractive cities.

"Wake up!" should my American friend, throwing some gravel in the general direction of the famous black swans. "Wake up, goddammit, there's tourists here!"

The black swans, till then sleeping peacefully on the ornamental pool, set up a dismal squawking. I knew how they felt; I, too, have been awakened at 1.30 a.m.

"I wonder how they keep them here," said the American, "there's nothing to stop them flying away."

"Probably the pond is too small," I suggested. "You know how much space even a lighter bird needs to get air-borne." "They could use the runways!"

In Perth I met one of the hundred thousand migrants to arrive each year.

"Before I came," he said, "I kept hearing about how careful I'd have to be if I didn't want to be called a Pommie bastard and have my face bashed in. And how I mustn't make jokes about manacle marks on wrists, because they're touchy about being descended from convicts. It nearly put me off coming. After all, you like to feel you'll be welcome. But do you know," he continued, "I never seem to meet any Aussies." He instanced his home suburb where Australians were outnumbered ten to one, mainly by British migrants, helped out by Spanish, Italian and Greek settlers.

"I reckon the Aussies are a dying race," he concluded, "and they've got them somewhere in the outback on tribal reservations next to the Aborigines."

He then gave me his views on the treatment of the dwindling Aboriginal population.

"They aren't getting a fair go," he said. "This is supposed to be a democracy, so they should get the same pay for doing the same job, and how they spend their money - on grog or whatever - is their affair."

That evening a business acquaintance took me from his office to an R.S.L. club. (The Returned Services League is a nation-wide ex-servicemen's association.) There, without difficulty, I was able to bring the conversation round to the same issue.

"You've got to put some restrictions on them," said one florid character, rapping on the bar to attract the steward's attention, "they're like children - very primitive."

"That's true," agreed the man to his left. (To be strictly accurate, he said: "Thash true", but it was then almost nine o'clock and we had been at the bar since six.) "You can't trust them to use liquor sensibly, so, in their own interests you've got to restrict them."

"Same again, Captain?" enquired the steward, who, throughout the evening made a point of using the war-time rankings of the various ex-officers present. They did not seem to mind.

"Of course," said the florid man, "you can't pay them what you'll pay a white stockman, they're too unreliable. Just when you might need them, they'll 'go walkabout'."

This magic phrase, several times incanted, seemed to dispose of the equal pay issue and I respectfully asked for enlightenment.

So far as I could follow the explanation, "walkabout" is equivalent to the White's summer holiday. The Aboriginal stockman, after long, boring spells herding cattle in interminable areas of semi-desert, likes to go away for a change, and a chance to visit his relatives and tribe. The White Australian, after long, boring spells on factory assembly lines, likes to go away for a change, and a chance to visit his relatives and friends. Both are prepared to cover long distances; the one by car, the other on foot. For his "walkabout", the White uses his three weeks holiday, Christmas, New Year, Proclamation Day and sundry strikes.

Whether the Aussie is able to use liquor more responsibly than the Aboriginal, who can judge? It is true that he is in better practice, and has felt justified in progressively eliminating restrictions on his own drinking. The famous "six o'clock swill" has now disappeared in favour of a ten o'clock closing time.

Chapter 22 Adelaide

"Do you happen to know where I'd get a bit of labouring to do?" asked the burly Australian. I was standing in one of Adelaide's pleasant squares wondering which of the many parked cars was the one I had hired, and wishing I had noted its registration number.

"I'm sorry, I don't," I said.

"Wouldn't it make you bloody sick!" he ejaculated. "Our bloody Government bloody-well importing all these bloody 'refos' when Australians can't get work!"

Australia's unemployment is as low as anywhere in the world, but I have frequently observed how unlucky some of the unemployed contrive to be. I once gave a lift to a man who was heading for Scotland to see if there was any pea-picking. This was in December, and he was in Evesham where he had missed the fruit season by a bare three months. No doubt, in June, he would be doggedly pursuing snow-shifting jobs in London. How many of us, I wonder, would be prepared to try as hard?

"Refos?" I queried.

"Refugees, mate," he explained. "New Australians they're called now. You'd think somebody'd give a returned serviceman a break. Look, mate - you can see I'm no 'bum', but I've used my last money on a telegram to my sister in Perth. Could you let me have a few shillings for a meal?"

I handed him two twenty cent pieces.

"Can you spare another one and I can have a drink too:" I doled out one more.

"Give me your address so I can let you have it back."

"That's all right", I said, adding the magic phrase which I have always found much appreciated by self-respecting mendicants: "You'd do as much for me!"

"Too bloody right, mate," he cried, grasping my hand. "Look, you're a 'pom' aren't you? Well, as soon as I'm in funds, I'll give this to some other pommie be- bloke, that is. How will that be?"

This incident was completely exceptional. Australians are an independent race who refuse tips, and do not cadge or beg. The same trait makes the "dinkum Aussie" untrainable to jobs involving personal service. An Australian asked to wait at table is as nervous and uneasy as a racehorse in the shafts of a cart. He will grimly slap a plate of steak and eggs in front of the diner, mutter: "There y'are mate," and stump off. Hotel service has now been taken over by New Australians, to the relief of all parties. Similarly, the Aussie barber who talked fishing as he sheared his cobber with a few deft strokes learned in the shearing-sheds, is almost defunct. In his place stands the Italian hair-stylist, who is prepared to turn out his teen-age clients looking like Beatles, if that is what they want, and will use the occasion to practise his English.

Adelaide, I had read, is the "Athens of the Southern Hemisphere", and the "City of Light" - a punning-reference to its founder, Colonel Light, though when I tried this "City of Light" tag on an inhabitant, it failed to register.

It is a gracefully attractive city, lying between the lovely Adelaide Hills and the sea, and has one of the best climates on earth - about 2,500 hours of sunshine yearly, low humidity, and most of its 25 inches annual rainfall in the mild, short winters. I found, however, that the people there like to believe that the winters are particularly vicious, and from two separate sources I heard of a Scots girl who said she had never felt so cold in Scotland as here. The third time I heard the story, it was a girl from Alaska, and had I stayed, no doubt I would have heard of an Eskimo dying of exposure there.

North of Adelaide is the desert from which on occasion hot winds sweep down like a blast from a furnace. This is a region of scrub and rock in which the eye looks for something green to rest it from the shimmering expanses of red, yellow and blue - but does not find it; and where lakes contain no more water than the seas of the moon. Yet across this waste, as fearsome as any in the world, the ubiquitous Holden Utility (or "Ute") ploughs its way, raising dust clouds from the tracks, which linger in the oven-hot air long after the vehicle is out of earshot. The driver and his companions may be heading a thousand miles across the interior, to or from Queensland. Motorists have died when their cars broke down, because they had not let it be known that they were travelling there or because they failed to stay with the car and wandered off into a trackless wilderness.

This, of course, no more deters the adventurous than the occasional fatality stops mountaineering or spear-fishing - perhaps it is the secret of their popularity.

In this region are Woomera (the rocket range) and the largest fields of opals in the world. As in many parts of Australia, place names are of Aboriginal derivation and are pleasantly euphonious, suggesting this sort of verse:

Lyric.
In Andamooka's opal fields
My love and I did lie.
We lay the whole night long beneath
An opalescent sky.
We left as lights of Woomera
Waned with the desert dawn;
Coober-Pedy, Oodnadatta
Beckoned us that morn.
Now on the Birdsville Track we speed, I and my love - my beaut!
My cobber, mate, my all-in-all –
My dusty Holden "Ute."

Chapter 23 Melbourne

On the plane to Melbourne, I sat by a man who described it as combining the worst aspects of British weather, Victorian morality, and Tokyo traffic. It is true that the weather often runs the gamut of changes in the course of a day, and by contrast with Adelaide's blue sea, the water in Port Phillip Bay slops around greyly, but Melbourne, like Manchester, is much maligned. All over the world there is a belief that Mancurians live beneath a ceaseless drizzle, and the legend of Melbourne's weather is almost as widespread. It was interesting to find that hoary old jokes about Manchester have migrated to Australia and are told about Melbourne. The Yarra River is also the subject of local witticisms. It is described as the only "upside down" river - having its mud on top, and as being "too thick to swim in but too thin to plough."

Collins Street, seen first on a tranquil Sunday evening as the church bells were sonorously calling the faithful to prayer, conveyed an impression of calm dignity. The following morning the traffic transformed the street into a bedlam, but at the top, "Paris" end, where cafe tables out on the pavement are shaded by the trees, I enjoyed a coffee-break enlivened by a tall, gaunt and unshaven man at the next table.

Having finished his drink he stood to attention, then, without bending his knees, demonstrated that he could place his cup and saucer flat on the ground. Again standing rigidly to attention, he recited a tea "commercial" which I had been unfortunate enough to see on television the previous evening. He mimed with dreadful accuracy the mincing tones of the lady, though the striking contrast between the smooth, silly words and his mad appearance, distinctly added impact to the advertisement. The tea commercial was followed by two for cigarettes and two for soft drinks, and in all of them he seemed word-perfect.

As a waitress tried to get rid of him, he repeated his trick with the cup and saucer, this time accidentally dropping a half cigarette from his shirt pocket into the tea dregs. Before leaving he retrieved it and put it, sopping wet, back in his pocket. I was left to speculate on whether T.V. adverts had driven him out of his mind, or whether, because he was out of his mind, he enjoyed reciting them.

Chapter 24 Sydney

Before leaving for Sydney, I was assured that, as a sedate Briton, I would find it too noisy, brash and Americanised. The rivalry between the two cities is strong and the only point on which they are prepared to agree is that Adelaide is a graveyard.

The taxi-drivers of Sydney are a colourful and independent breed. The colour comes out in their language, which is the worst I have heard since my schooldays, and the independence shows in their attitude to their fares. The taxi driver insists on a man-to-man relationship, which is very generous of him since as a Sydneysider he knows himself your superior. To adapt an old saying: "You don't ask a man if he's from Sydney. If he is, he'll tell you, and if he's not - why embarrass him?"

Cities have their characteristic noises; in Bangkok it is the blaring of motor horns; in Sydney the howling of tortured tyres and brakes. This may be partly due to Australia's "give way to the right" rule. At a road-junction, or crossroads not controlled by signals, drivers must give way to traffic on their right. There is no distinction as such between major and minor roads; a car travelling at 50 m.p.h. along a main highway must expect to see vehicles come shooting out in front of him from obscure side-turnings on his right. In practice, few drivers are stupid enough to believe that drivers on the main highway will accord them their legal right of way. At crossroads, if vehicles have arrived simultaneously from the four directions, a position of stalemate is created, since each driver has traffic to his right and no-one can move.

There are enough exceptions and complications resulting from the prior rights of traffic on dual highways (unless intersected by a dual highway), to ensure that few drivers really understand the rule, and to help account for Australia's road toll which is relatively the second highest in the world, with over 3,000 deaths annually. This is some three thousand times more than the deaths due to sharks, but the sharks score heavily in terms of publicity. An alleged shark, allegedly taking dead fish from a skin-diver's float warrants space in Australia's only national daily paper.

The highlight of my stay in Sydney was a visit to a club which, at low cost provides its members with first-class facilities in spacious, wall-appointed premises, together with good food - all financed from the profits of dozens of Poker Machines, ranged round a large assembly room. There was strong opposition to these "one-armed bandits" from sections of the Churches and other groups, who consider them demoralising and responsible for much hardship and unhappiness. The stock reply to this is that nobody is under any compulsion to play the machines; members may make full use of the club facilities without ever putting in a single coin. Those who do are thus voluntarily subsidising poorer members. This, say the abolitionists, ignores the fact that gambling exerts an unwholesome fascination over many reasonably normal people, and that human beings were not designed to be unduly exposed to temptation.

For over two hours, I was part of a syndicate of four, taking turns to operate one machine. This system slows down the rate at which money can be lost and also averages out the luck, to some extent.

All types of "pull" were used on the machine, and for variety, one of our consortium would cover up the dials with his hand and operate blind, so that each time the dials had come to rest, there was a tense pause to find out if the music of coins shooting into the cup would be heard, or merely the final click announcing that another twenty-cent coin had gone for ever. Left-handed pulls were tried, violent snatches, imperceptibly slow pulls, a left-handed push action from an operator who had climbed behind the machine - anything in an attempt to fool it. All knew well that the machines could not lose, but here I saw in action the Australian "battler", whose philosophy it is that you cannot win, but you must keep on battling. A jackpot enabled our syndicate to finish operations without serious loss, but then one of the party wandered off to try his luck alone, and within an hour returned disconsolate having lost more than ten dollars.

Despite the forecast of my Melbourne friend, I found Sydney stimulating and enjoyed my few days there, partly no doubt, because I was taken around by a widely travelled Sydney man who communicated much of his own enthusiasm for the city.

Sydney has an abundance of small bays where sailing boats ride gently at anchor, tempting large numbers of art students to their artistic doom. It was interesting to walk past the painters and to look at their efforts, and it would have been a useful exercise for the artists themselves. Perhaps, in later life they would overcome the handicap, but on the evidence of their paintings, all had been ruined by over-exposure at an impressionable age, to the Impressionists. Other student groups on the grass bordering Rushcutters Bay, were strumming stringed instruments, and singing folk songs pleasantly.

At the cinema of Sydney University, I saw the Soviet film of "Hamlet". The soundtrack was in Russian of course, but English sub-titles gave Shakespeare's words. As the ghost of Hamlet's father was taking his leave, to the sub-titled words:

"Remember me!" - a cryptic message was superimposed on the screen, reading: "Will Miss Seisgy please go to the foyer." The laugh which this provoked somewhat destroyed the dramatic intensity of the scene but made it a Hamlet to remember.

Chapter 25 New Zealand

We flew to Christchurch in the late afternoon, across the ramparts of the Southern Alps, half in sun, half in shadow, with the 12,349 ft. mass of Mount Cook to the North. New Zealand is compact enough to be comprehended physically from the air, and the flights from Christchurch to Nelson, to Wellington and on to Auckland were worth all the geography books ever written.

"Windy" Wellington lies in the only break in the mountain chains of North and South Islands, and winds are funnelled through Cook Strait with accelerated velocity. Between November and April there are, on average, seventeen days when winds of 60 m.p.h. or more, are experienced, and there are 40 m.p.h. winds thrice weekly. There is a sort of parallel, pointed out to me by an Australian, between the cities of Sydney, Melbourne and Adelaide - and Auckland, Wellington and Christchurch. Sydney and Auckland are the big cities, both built around much water; Melbourne and Wellington have a reputation for bad weather, while Adelaide and Christchurch are the more leisurely and formally scenic cities.

Auckland is "Hobson's choice", built on a site chosen by Captain William Hobson, who intended that it should be the Capital. It is the only city I observed to have female taxi-drivers, who, incidentally, must cease work at dusk, though it was not made clear whether this was for their own protection or their customers.

My hotel followed the old custom of seating guests in the dining-room at specific tables, rather than leaving them free to wander round and pick the table with the prettiest waitress. At breakfast I sat opposite a man in the milk business, with a problem caused by Holstein cows in Christchurch giving milk, ample in quantity, but deficient in certain prescribed milk-solids, I said: "You will have to take the bull by the horns and demand better milk." Perhaps it was too early in the day, because he answered: "It's not quite as simple as that. We don't want to force anyone out of business."

New Zealand is called "A world in miniature." For anyone not contaminated by the bustle and artificiality of big cities, it offers a leisurely, almost idyllic existence, and the tourists are catered for with clean, comfortable hotels and everything they should require in the way of variety of activity and scene. The weather ranges from sub-tropical in Auckland province, to the extreme of the foulest weather imaginable, on the West Coast of South Island if visited at the wrong time.

One man's brief stay there included, he said, five inches of snow, twelve inches of hail, thirteen inches of rain, and plagues of mosquitoes, sand-flies and blow-flies.

Many on holiday were Australians, who make repeated trips across the Tasman Sea to check that New Zealand is still inferior to their own country. In this remote part of the globe, Australia is a powerful neighbour, and New Zealand may have some private apprehensions about her ability of survive separately. A Christchurch man described Australians as "like rough, uncultured New Zealanders, if you can imagine such a thing," but a stranger to both countries would find great difficulty in sorting out the one from the other. Even the accents are very similar.

A visit to Rotorua took me through country which seemed effortlessly and unfailingly beautiful; even the cloud formations were spectacular. Rotorua itself was something of an anticlimax, and once it had been explained to me that the hot springs and the steam chugging from the ground resulted from water on a natural bed of hot ash, it all seemed inevitable. My bedroom, like the rest of Rotorua, smelt of sulphur. I slept badly, dreaming that I was in Hell and unable to get an exit-visa.

CHAPTER 26
The United States of America

"Before you leave for the U.S.A.," said a friend, "insure against sickness. Medical treatment there, costs the earth." He knew someone, perfectly fit normally, but overtired, who passed out in a New York hotel and owed two hundred dollars by the time he was on his feet again, ten minutes later.

At Sydney Airport I was too busy to buy insurance, because I wanted to take some duty-free liquor to the U.S.A.

"What do Americans drink, usually?" I asked the man behind the counter.

"Anything that's put in front of them, mostly," he answered, and having enjoyed his little jest, he became helpful and sold me five bottles of assorted whiskies and gin. Before I got rid of these, I called at Honolulu, Los Angeles, Memphis and New York, and soon felt like Sinbad with the Old Man of the Sea on his back, because I had to manhandle the bag of bottles in addition to my own hand-baggage. No-one, unless equipped with more than the usual complement of arms should attempt to travel with over two pieces of luggage.

Until the main suitcase is reclaimed from Baggage-Collection, one hand is free for proffering passport, disembarkation-card, health-documents, Customs-declaration, currency-forms and other papers. The passenger who ignores this natural limitation may be seen carrying his passport between bared teeth, like a dog delivering newspapers.

Apart from this nuisance and the considerable weight of five bottles of spirits, there was the risk of smashing them.

The transition from the pressurised jet-plane to the different, temperature of the airports, causes condensation on the surface of bottles which then rot the paper carrier-bag and crash to the ground. At one Airport we had all waded through a pool of whisky in (not inappropriately) - the Health Department, resulting from a tragic accident of this sort, to two bottles of Scotch.

In the 16th Century, Howell wrote of those who "travel much but see little, like Jonah in the whale's belly." By the time I reached Los Angeles on Monday morning, after crossing the Pacific Ocean at an altitude of 30,000 ft. in a Boeing's belly, I knew what Howell meant. I had had a weekend consisting of two Saturdays and a Sunday, had spent two nights out of the three, in 'planes and had advanced my watch several times, by amounts of two or three hours, so that my only link with Sydney time was the state of my stubble.

Sandwiched between my night-flight from Sydney and my night-flight to Los Angeles, was a forty-hour stop-over in Honolulu, which I spent mainly swimming, or sleeping on the beach near my Waikiki hotel. Within its grounds is a huge banyan tree, beneath whose shade Robert Louis Stevenson wrote.

Although Hawaii is one of the States of the U.S.A., and though its inhabitants speak not of "going to the U.S.A." but of "going to the mainland," this is a kindly gesture which need deceive no-one. The U.S.A. is still more than two thousand miles away.

Memphis

Los Angeles Airport in the early morning was like a vast concrete temple. The transfer to a flight for Memphis meant a few hours wait at the Airport, but not enough time to visit the city. By following various signs, I reached a point from which coaches would leave "every ten minutes" for the domestic terminal.

"What a fine thing American efficiency is!" I thought. "It is easy to sneer at it, but how refreshing after the delays and evasions of the Orient."

Forty minutes later, still without a coach, I had modified my thinking somewhat. When eventually transferred to the domestic departure-lounge, I wanted first to park the bag of spirits which was then depressing my own. Admirably, next to the safe-deposit lockers were some machines offering coins for dollars, and suggesting the reinsertion of any rejected bill since the machine may on occasion, throw out perfectly good notes. After all six of my one-dollar bills had been several times ejected, I appealed to a small boy, who put them through again, still unsuccessfully. Then he kicked the machine twice, shook it violently and announced that it was out of order, which now seemed most probable. I finally got change by the old-fashioned method of asking the friendly cashier at the coffeeshop, who produced eight shining new quarters.

One of these enabled me to leave my bottles in a safe-deposit. Next, I applied myself to the task of obtaining postage-stamps for some cards I had written. I found a stamp-machine and noted with a sense of outrage that someone was making a profit on the stamps since they came packaged at a price higher than their face value. To an Englishman there is something almost sacred about stamps, but a little reflection convinced me that this was an irrational view. My next feeling was one of regret that I had not done Calculus and could not workout the cheapest permutation which would make up the eleven-cent postage on each of four cards.

The machines offered:

For 50 cents, 1-30c and 2-5c stamps (value 40 cents)

For 25 cents, 1-15c and 1-5c stamp (value 20 cents) or

1-11c and 1-8c stamp (value 19 cents) or
3-6c and 2-1c stamps (value 20 cents) or
2-8c and 1-4c stamp (value 20 cents) or
5-4c stamps (value 20 cents) or
4-5c stamps (value 20 cents)

It seemed to me that I would spend more than necessary and end up with a lot of unwanted stamps. At a venture, I put in a quarter and pulled the lever to get one 11c and one 8c stamp, even though at 19c this was the worst value. They arrived in a little cardboard folder, saying on the one side: "Sanitarily Packaged -Save a Trip to Post Office" and on the other side: "You look on the bright side of most things and have a thankful heart." The next folder said: "There will be much good fortune and you will be appreciative and sharing," which seemed ambiguous as well as slightly menacing.

After posting the cards, I ran the gauntlet of machines offering cigarettes, machines offering food and drink, machines offering to copy documents, or shine shoes, or provide change - to the haven of the cafe where I could relax with a few of my own species.

In the U.S.A., the captain is inadequate if he can merely fly an aeroplane; he is expected to be an entertainer too, and over the P.A. system came a stream of witticisms such as:

"Our flight should take an hour-and-a-half in good round figures - and talking of good round figures, your hostesses today are……."

"We are a fresh crew- I use the word loosely."

"We have gone into a slightly elliptical circling orbit as we do not yet have ground-clearance to land. I felt I should mention this, in case you thought we were hopelessly lost."

I doubt whether this is good Public Relations; we like to think of the Captain as a serious, dedicated man, seated with eyes constantly on the instruments, except for swift glances to port and starboard to verify that both wings are intact and that none of the engines is on fire. A flippant Captain gave me the same sense of unease as when, a few weeks later, in a bar outside Toronto Airport, my companion said: "Look, there's the crew of your 'plane getting 'tanked up'." It was a very dark bar I had jocularly been offered a 'seeing-eye' dog on entering and across the gloom I could just see peaked caps. But it was a slander; they were Air Force officers.

My captains should be humourless men, addicted to nothing stronger than weak tea. The hostesses can provide glamour, and the passengers can drink the hard liquor. The captain is there to fly the aeroplane - and let us have no levity, please.

That evening I dined at a hotel overlooking the Mississippi at Memphis, surrounded by rich Southern accents; and surely, as the sun disappeared and darkness stole across the river, the raft of Tom and Huck emerged from the rushy margins and edged into the mainstream.

Later, my host drove some distance to my motel, pulling up in front of one of a number of tumbledown, wooden shacks in a clearing. This was his regular joke and I "fell" for it. With dismay in my heart, I uttered a few polite insincerities about the pleasant surroundings, and he then drove on to the real motel, a few miles away, which was as good as I found anywhere.

Chicago

The following day I flew to Chicago, though after slogging through the interminable corridors of O'Hare Airport, my impression was that I had walked the distance. Chicago, of course, was different from my preconceived ideas; not that I was expecting gangsters, but I anticipated a noisy, ultramodern city situated, as a boy at my school once wrote, "at the bottom of Lake Michigan."

The noise and bustle are there, but so too are pleasant suburbs, attractive lakeside drives, and ornately old-style bars reminiscent of the Chicago of Dreiser's novels. Even the hotel I stayed at, the Pick Congress, was sedate, luxurious and traditional in style.

The fault lies mainly with our school-books which since 1492 or thereabout, have continued to speak of the "New World", ignoring the fact that the centuries have been rolling by. Buildings, during a period of two or three hundred years are pulled down, or burn down, or fall down and there is nothing old under the sun. I always feel cheated when visiting an old edifice, allegedly built in the 12th Century and find instead that: "This historic building was constructed in 1740 on what was presumed to be the site of the original foundation of 1190 A.D. It was extended in 1780 and 1790, restored in 1860 and completely gutted by fire in 1910. The present structure (housing a Division of the N.C.B.) was completed in 1935, about two miles from the former site and is a reproduction, based on an artist's impression made on Armistice Night, 1918, of what the original may have looked like, prior to, or possibly just after the fire."

New York

Near Philadelphia I ate several times at the "Buck", an old inn which reminded me strongly of one particular English Inn, but when I revisited the Cheshire inn I found it converted into a sort of motel. Because the Americans also regard themselves as a new country, they cherish their older properties. When I light-heartedly made an offer for Philadelphia's Liberty Bell, based on its value as scrap iron, I realised from the stony silence that this was a joke in poor taste. There was a feeling of newness in some of the Australian cities, though even there, Sydney has a castle and some of its narrow streets off the city centre have an old-fashioned air about them. But America is far too old to masquerade any longer as the New World. It is as unseemly as a matron in mini-skirts.

In New York I fell asleep in the office of a Director of the Company we both work for, and though with ready presence of mind he threw a box of paper-clips at me, he did not seem to care.

In fact, thanks to an article in Readers' Digest, it is now widely understood that a businessman who falls asleep all over the place is not, as was previously assumed, a dissolute waster who has been racketing around the town all night, but a man whose inner-clock has been disturbed by the rigours of speeding across time-zones. The jet-propelled businessman is later free to snore peacefully anywhere and at any time, sure of sympathetic understanding. In a colleague's garden, near Philadelphia as I was dozing off, I heard lowered voices commenting on the terrible strain of flying. I had, that afternoon, arrived by train from New York, but who was I to contradict them?

New York's skyscrapers are awe-inspiring and, like the statues and monoliths of a long-vanished society, provoke the question, what manner of people built these? The mystery deepens after an examination of the shops, where everything is for sale - everything but intangibles such as tranquillity, love and friendship. Even these, by implication, are offered as the reward of buying deodorant, detergent, battery-powered back-scratchers, bar-stool safety-belts, and bedroom mood-indicators with settings on the dial such as: "Coax me", "Too tired", "Now about that mink!", "Too late", and "If I'm not back in ten minutes, start without me."

I travelled the Subway to Bronx Botanical Gardens to hear a Saturday Open-Air Concert, given by the New York Philharmonic Symphony Orchestra. Bronx Botanical Gardens deserve to be remembered as the site of a historic discovery by the Curator, Mr. Davis, which was reported thus:

"Gorillas in Bronx Zoo are encouraged to watch T.V. 'It keeps them quiet', says Mr. Joseph Davis. The gorillas, whose ages range from six to seventeen used to bicker incessantly. Now, they sit calmly together watching the screen through the bars of their cage."

The final step obviously is to remove the bars and then, hand in hand, humans and gorillas all, we can watch together.

The concert included the Meistersingers Overture and Beethoven's Choral Symphony, and was heard by thousands of people, black and white, seated on the grass. The conductor, William Steinberg, wore a beret against the strong sun, which gave him a rakish look. Many ruminant policemen patrolled the park, idly twirling their clubs. Presumably the authorities were nervous because of race-riots a few days earlier in other cities. But there was no trouble; black and white dotted the grass indiscriminately, listening peaceably to Beethoven's setting of Schiller's "Ode to Joy", whose words; "Alle Menschen werden Prüden", still ring out with dignity and conviction.

Saucon Valley Country Club is at Bethlehem, Pennsylvania and I accompanied four golfers there, one sunny Sunday. To the best of my recollection, two of them were called Walt and two Ed, but it may have been the other way round. As we drove through the lovely countryside from Philadelphia, some quiet boasting was going on in the car and I looked forward to seeing good golf. The grounds were magnificent, the weather good, and I was happy to walk and at the request of one of the Walts, to take cine shots of his golf action.

The score-card, still in my possession suggests that all of them had a bad day. "Par", for the nine holes out is 36, and the card shows 52, 54, 57 and 69. The return nine holes took 53, 58, 52 and 57, again with a "par" of 36. The reel of film I exposed must have looked like scenes from "Lawrence of Arabia" as clouds of sand ware hacked into the air from trap after trap. I never heard how the film turned out.

At this stage in my visit to the U.S.A. 1 had overcome the initial language problem and had learned the dozen or so phrases making up the local patois. The purpose of these is to enable a speaker with nothing to say, to continue talking, and since there is only one socially acceptable way of saying anything, an illusion of democratic "togetherness" is created. Each word or phrase serves for dozens of different expressions, thus eliminating those irritating shades of meaning in which the English language abounds.

"Configuration", for instance, is always used for "shape", "design" or a number of other alternatives, and has the advantage of being longer than any of them. At a meeting I attended, an engineer said: "We may have to do something about it configurationwise."

"As long as" may mean "since", "as", "while", "when" if or even "as long as", and should soon replace about six of the old Parts of Speech. "Right now" is just a noise. "The time right now is a quarter of four" means: "It's quarter to four." In the sentence: "She had herself a ball", "a ball" means a good time, or about four hundred alternatives. I heard of a girl who had "a ball of a party", and had I stayed longer might have been told that someone had a "ball of a ball". "She's a doll!" is the standardised description of any female still with pretentious to youth, and not demonstrably ugly. "Right." means "yes", or "that's, true", or "I understand", or "I certainly agree with you!" according to the intonation, and proves that the listener has not fallen asleep or gone away.

Thus, I was quickly able to translate: "As long as you're going to the bar, why don't I join you there?" - as, "I'll meet you in the bar." This "why don't I?" construction can, however, be confusing. In Singapore I saw a waiter continue standing patiently, after receiving an order: "Why don't I just have a double order of pancakes with maple syrup, and some black coffee?" The waiter, thinking that the American was communing with himself, was waiting for the result of this auto-interrogation.

It was also in Singapore that I suddenly realised that I was hearing an American version of "Oh, to be in England, now that April's there!" The American was sitting slumped over a bar, stirring the pack-ice in his drink with an abstracted forefinger, and his "Home Thoughts from Abroad", voiced to a sympathetic compatriot, went like this:

"Why don't I take some leave,
And visit with my folks,
As lawng as things are quiet
Businesswise.
(Compatriot: "Too goddam quiet, if you ask me!")
"You sure get goddam sick
Of the humidity here.
For my money the place stinks,
Climatewise."
(Compatriot: "You can say that again!")
"Brother! What wouldn't I give
 To be in N.J. right now.
Things will be looking real nice
Scenerywise."
(Compatriot: "That's for sure!")

Arid now, effectively, my journey was finished. To the East lay England, and once more I could believe in its existence. For the first fortnight of my tour, I had felt mentally disorientated, and conscious always of my remoteness from home.

Then, by a sudden shift of its axis, the world again revolved around me and continued this comforting practice throughout my wanderings. England became no more than a convenient intellectual concept, incapable of proof. In a play I once read, the dead lived again, during those brief and ever less frequent moments when the living spoke of them. Similarly, family and friends would be with me fleetingly in Rangoon, in Christchurch, or in Memphis, evoked by a phrase in a letter, a familiar object, or something of the sort. Apart from these briefly glowing points of illumination, all was a vast darkness and even Bishop Berkeley had ceased to exist. I had brought family photographs with me, but destroyed them when I found myself remembering the photograph and not the person.

After one of his epic lone voyages across the world, Francis Chichester commented that when, far out at sea, he played some of his favourite music, it made him so unutterably sad that he played it no more that trip. Thinking about this, he decided that during an enterprise of that sort, faculties not essential to success hibernated, and that music, by reminding him of the dormant aspects of his personality, made him unhappy.

His, of course, was an extreme case, since he was living with danger, physical stress and solitude, but even I felt now as though emerging from a dreary winter, so prolonged that no memory of other seasons remained - into a bounteous May.

Recently my harmonica playing had been confined to "Home, Sweet Home", partly, it is true, because it is easy to play, but also because its melancholy mood matched my own. As time went by, "Home, Sweet Home" became slower in tempo, more plaintive, more dirge—like, and once as I had the last anguished notes by the throat, I heard a burst of violent sobbing from the next room, followed by a single revolver shot.

From Philadelphia to New York again, and by air to Buffalo with a colleague, for a meeting in Batavia. Then a sunny drive through tranquil countryside to the shore of Lake Ontario and along it to Niagara. The wide horizons and rural scene reminded me of past journeys through Lincolnshire. When I said this to my companion he pointed out on his map the names Welland and Grimsby, so the early settlers had clearly seen the resemblance too. We stopped to buy apples and plums from a roadside stall and to drink tea. After a period of city life I was in a mood to appreciate the change, and my colleague seemed to be enjoying the escape from his New York office.

We stayed the night at the town of Niagara, apparently the only couple not on a honeymoon, and the next morning crossed into Canada. After business calls in St. Catherine's and Toronto, I boarded my 'plane and a few hours later was back in London.

THE END

EPILOGUE

This narrative should have ended at London Airport, with a welcome back by the Chairman of the Company, who by the felicitous phrase "we Directors" would announce the wanderer's elevation to the Board. Unaccountably this did not happen. The Export Director had transferred himself from his bar in the City to the Cocktail Lounge at the Airport, but he almost missed me. Overlooking the fact that two excuses are less convincing than one, he explained that he had not heard the announcement of my 'plane's arrival, and that he had not wished to intrude on the welcome of my family. There was no mention of a directorship. Instead, before parting he said:

"You're going to want time to sort yourself out and let your family see something of you. But next week there's a Convention we'd like you to attend. It just means a couple of days in Harrogate. You'll find it a bit dull after places like Bangkok, but someone has to go and as you're already disorganised, it's better than disrupting anyone else. At any rate you'll find it a nice dull way of unwinding after your travels. You can't get into trouble in Harrogate."

This sort of statement offers a direct challenge to Fate, and inevitably I found myself a week later on a remote Yorkshire moor, beneath a cold drizzle, wondering how on earth the loss of a Company car could be explained without leading to the inference that I had taken leave of my senses.

It had started innocently enough. I had a two-hour break between Conference Papers and rather than returning to my hotel for lunch, decided on a quick sandwich and a drive to Ilkley Moor. It seemed a pity to miss the chance of standing on this famous moor "ba t'at." The road, according to the map, was secondary with a short middle section in dual dotted lines which I took to mean an unmetalled road.

It turned out to be a rough track which unexpectedly ran down a steep hill and turned itself into a stream where the car became bogged. I looked again at the map and noticed a peculiar symbol which, on reference to the key, I now learned indicated a swamp. Yes, this was it. For miles I had driven across desolate moorland, bare of human or animal life, and help was a long way from me, but if I could get the car on to the heather at the side, I could drive back up the hill to firm track.

The underside of the chassis rested on the ground, and only under the rear bumper-bracket was there space for the jack. At first the base of the jack would disappear into the mud as I twisted the handle, in conformity with the law of mechanics which says that to every action there is an equal and opposite reaction, and only after repeated packing with stones was a base provided, firm enough to allow the car to be raised.

Surprisingly, loose stones were scarce, and I had to waste time searching the heather for enough to pack under the wheels. After an hour-and-a-half of hand-blistering, back-breaking work, the car was raised on stone piles but as soon as I tried to drive to firm ground, all the stones shot from beneath the spinning wheels and the car settled down once more in the mud.

It required two more attempts and over two hours of labour before the car stood high and dry on the heather, but now it refused to climb the steep gradient. The engine was firing on three cylinders only, because a plug lead had broken loose, but I was by then incapable of rational thought and did not discover till next day the reason for the loss of power. The only alternative seemed to be to drive on as the track or stream should shortly link up with a metalled road on the other side of this Slough of Despond. It was dark and I had to reconnoitre on foot, setting up the jack-handle with a handkerchief tied to it, as a mark, every few dozen yards ahead of the car, so that I could drive to it, but after a few repetitions of this manoeuvre I realised that there was no way through for a car. All around were ditches and boggy streamlets. After reversing to a safe position on dry heather, I meticulously locked the car and set out to walk the eight or nine miles to Ilkley, whose lights were just visible. But now my Guardian Angel suddenly awoke to my predicament, stopped the rain, drew back the clouds obscuring the moon and stood by for further action.

At one point I walked towards a road, shining in the moonlight, only to find it a river, but the detour this forced on me brought me out on a road close to a petrol-station, and though no taxi was locally available, the last 'bus from Ilkley to Harrogate obligingly rolled up within minutes and soon I was back at my hotel, plastered with mud, too weary to eat, too weary to sleep and wondering if the car could ever be recovered.

Next morning, with a breakdown-lorry from a Harrogate garage, I retraced my steps. Though not feeling in a very strong position to give advice to the driver, I said, with a deprecating laugh: "Better watch it down here. There's my car at the bottom, and this track is just mud down below." He nodded wisely, drove down and became bogged. Slowly he got out, slowly unloaded a shovel and passed it to his youthful mate. While he was poking around with it in a half-hearted fashion, I discovered the stray plug-lead in my car, fixed it, and then suggested to the breakdown gang that they prepared to give me a push while I tried to drive up. This time it worked. It was a hair-raising experience because I stayed on the heather and had to dodge small boulders which could have wrecked the suspension or steering.

We were now mobile and I drove our party several miles to a telephone so that the driver could speak to his garage and explain why he needed a bigger lorry and some help. He emerged disconsolate from the telephone box. I understood from his few laconic words in Yorkshire dialect that his equally Yorkshire boss had, in effect, told him not to be such an idle swine, but to get himself out with the equipment on his lorry. We were conveniently to an inn, and after drinks we returned. At their suggestion I left them after paying the break-down fee, and over-tipping them from feelings of guilt. But they had company, and the sun which had followed me on my travels broke through as they walked down to their stranded lorry.

There I left them, and in the words of the old story-books: "for aught that 1 know, they are there to this very day."

www.ingramcontent.com/pod-product-compliance
Lightning Source LLC
Chambersburg PA
CBHW052359220526
45465CB00003BB/1168